The art of the diva

Muzio Callas Olivero

D1564270

with valuable assistance from Clifford Elkin

Discographies compiled
by John Hunt

CONTENTS

The Art of the Diva
Published by John Hunt.
© 1997 John Hunt
reprinted 2009
ISBN 978-1-901395-00-6

Published 1997 by John Hunt

Copyright 1997   John Hunt

Sole distributors:
Travis & Emery,
17 Cecil Court,
London, WC2N 4EZ,
United Kingdom.
(+44) 20 7 459 2129.
sales@travis-and-emery.com

ACKNOWLEDGEMENT

This publication has been made possible by contributions and advance
subscriptions from the following

Richard Ames, New Barnet
Stefano Angeloni, Frasso Sabino
Yoshihiro Asada, Osaka
Jack Atkinson, Tasmania
Bruno Barthelmé, Le Creusot
E.C. Blake, York
J. Camps-Ros, Barcelona
J. Charrington, Cardiff
Eduardo Chibas, Caracas
Robert Christoforides, Fordingbridge
A. Copeman, Cambridge
F. De Vilder, Bussum
Richard Dennis, Greenhithe
John Derry, Newcastle-upon-Tyne
Hans-Peter Ebner, Milan
Bill Flowers, London
Henry Fogel, Chicago
T. Foley, Cork
Peter Fu, Hong Kong
Nobuo Fukumoto, Hamamatsu
Peter Fulop, Toronto
James Giles, Sidcup
Philip Goodman, London
Jean-Pierre Goossens, Luxembourg
Johann Gratz, Vienna
Peter Hammann, Bochum
Michael Harris, London
Tadashi Hasegawa, Nagoya
Naoya Hirabayashi, Tokyo
Martin Holland, Sale
John Hughes, Brisbane
Bodo Igesz, New York
Richard Igler, Vienna
Eugene Kaskey, New York
Shiro Kawai, Tokyo

Rodney Kempster, Basingstoke
Detlef Kissmann, Solingen
Eric Kobe, Lucerne
Elisabeth Legge-Schwarzkopf DBE, Zürich
John Mallinson, Hurst Green
Carlo Marinelli, Rome
Finn Moeller Larsen, Virum
Philip Moores, Stafford
Bruce Morrison, Gillingham
W. Moyle, Ombersley
Alan Newcombe, Hamburg
Hugh Palmer, Chelmsford
Jim Parsons, Sutton Coldfield
Laurence Pateman, London
James Pearson, Vienna
Tully Potter, Billericay
Peter Pugson, Buxton
Phil Rees, Pewsey
Patrick Russell, Calstock
Yves Saillard, Mollie-Margot
T. Scanes, Ashford
Neville Sumpter, Northolt
Yoshihiko Suzuki, Tokyo
H.A. Van Dijk, Apeldoorn
Mario Vicentini, Cassano Magnano
Hiromitsu Wada, Chiba
Urs Weber, St Gallen
G. Wright, Romford
Ken Wyman, Brentwood
Masakasu Abe, Chiba City
Helger Steinhauff, Stemwede
John Larsen, Mariager
Valery Ryvkin, New York

The art of the diva

Dictionary definitions of the term
"diva" refer simply to a great
female singer, a prima donna and,
in the original Italian, to a
goddess. The trappings of celebrity
which inevitably go with this
particular category of musical
practitioner attract, or seemingly
demand, an entire gamut of less
positive human characteristics:
vanity, jealousy, unreliability and
countless other colourful traits.
Yet much less has always been made
of the virtues needed for a star
performer to reach the top - selfless
dedication, iron discipline and
sheer hard work - and then required,
in even greater proportions, in order
to remain at that peak.

In fact no voice category is without
its divas or their masculine
equivalents - think of tenors like
Caruso, Corelli and Pavarotti or
basses like Chaliapin and Christoff.
The private life sometimes seemed
to reflect the colourful antics of
the operatic characters which these
artists would portray on stage.
Nevertheless, it was, and perhaps
always will be, the sopranos who
claim the limelight, ranging from
the coloraturas (from the
legendary Luisa Tetrazzini to
Kathleen Battle in our own times)
to the dramatic heavyweights (like
Helen Traubel and Birgit Nilsson).

Nowhere has the competition for fame
and notoriety been as intense as in
that central soprano area where
descriptions like lyric, spinto and
youthful dramatic apply. These are
the operatic voices who seem to
reign and suffer the most intensely,
who enjoy the greatest moments of
rapture and triumph, and then of
despair and degradation - in
whichever order the operatic scenario
might require.

Without doubt one of the most vivid
names from the more distant operatic
past (in gramophone terms, that is)
remains that of **Claudia Muzio**, a star
both in Europe and America for
several decades. The almost perfect
personification of the spinto voice
- a description which reference books
tell us is a lyric voice of
particular vigour and attack - is
represented on records by a good
cross-section of her repertory
(from Bellini to Recife) captured
in Muzio's prime (Edison and Pathé,
1915-1925) as well as from the Indian
summer (Columbia, 1934-1935) before
her early death in 1936. Virtually
the entire recorded output is brought
together on a set of Romophone CDs,
which also include the added treasure
of a glimpse of the soprano live on
stage in 1932 as Tosca.

Magda Olivero might appear, at first
sight, to be the very antithesis of
a diva, with her seemingly happy
disposition and secure family life.
Her early career in the 1930s, just
at the time when Muzio was taking
her leave, was firmly based on the
spinto schooling (Liù, Mimì and
Violetta in early Cetra recordings)
but gave way, after a period of
retirement and at the behest of the
composer Francesco Cilea, to a unique
dedication to verismo opera. This
is a field which can be so dangerous
for a lesser singer with faulty or
incomplete technique but which, in
Olivero's case, yielded unforgettably
concentrated and exhilarating
impersonations of Cilea's Adriana,
Mascagni's Iris, an entire gallery
of Puccini heroines and modern cameos
by composers such as Rosellini,
Menotti, Malipiero and Poulenc.

Shamefully neglected by the big record companies, Olivero's voice was captured in radio broadcasts and by in-house tapists. At the forefront of these, both for the quality of interpretation and sound, are a long series of performances, with complete operas as well as aria selections, organised by Dutch Radio in the 1960s. Yet even the least adequate among the other (amateur) recordings afford invaluable glimpses of a stage presence supported by a rock-steady technique: characteristic, singing "off the words" (which is more than clarity of diction) seems to heighten the visceral thrill. I can think of only one Olivero successor in this respect, and that is the under-valued British soprano Josephine Barstow.

Attending a Magda Olivero recital in the autumn of her career left me with indelible memories. It was in Paris in 1980, by which time she had devised a programme which she shared with a solo pianist. Although this recital contained more French and Italian song than it did opera, the inevitable Adriana and Manon Lescaut arias were not missing, carefully placed towards the end of the evening to give the effect of well-deserved encores. And it was indeed a long evening, starting late but not finishing much short of midnight, whereupon Olivero took a chair backstage and proceeded to chat to visitors and sign autographs until well past two in the morning! How far removed can one get from the aloof image of traditional prima donna?

Which leaves **Maria Callas**. In the case of no other singer whom one might have experienced repeatedly on stage is it more necessary, I feel, to allow a sufficient passage of time to elapse in order to temper one's judgement and to help achieve a true perspective. So overwhelmingly intense was the stage presence that we were left temporarily unfocussed, even unreceptive to the qualities of other deserving singers of the same repertoire. As an adoring member of the Callas audience I have to confess that for years after I was unwilling to concede that Sutherland or Tebaldi could offer anything comparable. From the London "Traviata" which was my first experience of Maria Callas in 1958 to the 1973 London concerts of that controversial farewell tour I was, quite literally, in a thrall. Were those first impressions the most telling ones?

An incredible sensibility to the meaning and colour of the text, and the transference of this to the music (Callas was an articulate speaker about these matters, as in her recorded discussions with the American musicologist Edward Downes), came from her utter identification with to the background and character of the person she was portraying. Immersal in rehearsals was so deep that she sometimes drew resentment from colleagues who were less conscientious than she herself.

From early stage experience a heavyweight among sopranos (roles like Leonore, Brünnhilde, Isolde and Kundry, with Santuzza and Tosca thrown in), Callas worked under Tullio Serafin's guidance towards bel canto (Puritani, Norma, Lucia), bringing such parts a greater dramatic profile than would have been possible from a purely coloratura background.

The Callas voice was difficult to
categorise - indeed it was claimed
that she possessed several quite
different ones - and this was a
factor, along with the voice's lack
of "beauty" in the traditional sense,
which divided the critics throughout
her tempestuous career.

So rich is the treasure-house of
surviving recordings that many of
the roles which Maria Callas made her
own are documented by performances
from the various stages of her
continuing development. Tosca, for
example, is heard in 12 more or less
complete versions recorded between
1950 and 1965, Norma in 10 between
1953 and 1965 and Traviata in 7
between 1951 and 1958.

In the cases of both Maria Callas
and Magda Olivero, the proliferation
of issues of the live (originally
pirate) material shows no sign of
abatement, making it nigh impossible
to produce a listing of catalogue
numbers which could claim to be
complete. I am therefore always
eager to hear from collectors who
can add to the information which I
have supplied in these discographies.

John Hunt

Claudia Muzio
1889 -1936

Discography compiled
by John Hunt

ALFRED BACHELET (1864-1944)

Chère nuit

New York November 1920	Orchestra Sodero	Edison 82218 LP: Esoteric (USA) 508 LP: Contrepoint (France) 20010 LP: OASI 565 LP: CBS Y 33793 LP: Rubini RS 310 CD: Pearl GEMMCDS 9072 CD: Cantabile BIM 7052 CD: Minerva MNA 31 CD: Romophone 810052

VINCENZO BELLINI (1801-1835)

Bianca e Fernando, excerpt (Sorgi, o padre!)

| New York
March 1922 | Orchestra
Sodero | Edison 82267
International Record Collectors Club 192
LP: London International TWV 91053
LP: Esoteric (USA) 502
LP: Contrepoint (France) 20009
LP: Scala (USA) 849
LP: OASI 565
LP: Top Artists' Platter 328
LP: Belcantodisc BC 202
LP: CBS Y 32676
LP: Rubini RS 310
CD: Pearl GEMMCDS 9072
CD: Cantabile BIM 7052
CD: Minerva MNA 31
CD: Romophone 810052 |

Norma, excerpt (Casta diva)

| Milan
June 1935 | Orchestra
and Chorus
Molajoli | 78: Columbia LX 622/LCX 23
78: Columbia (Italy) BQX 2502/BQX 2520
78: Columbia (Argentina) 264960
78: Columbia (USA) M 259/9165M
LP: Columbia COLC 101
LP: Columbia (USA) ML 4404
LP: Angel 60111
LP: EMI 3C 053 00923M/EX 29 01633
CD: EMI CDH 769 7902
CD: Romophone 810152 |

La sonnambula, excerpt (Ah non credea mirarti)

| Milan
June 1935 | Orchestra
Molajoli | 78: Columbia LCX 27
78: Columbia (Italy) BQX 2506/BQX 2522
78: Columbia (USA) M 259/9165M
LP: Columbia COLC 101
LP: Columbia (USA) ML 4404
LP: Angel 60111
LP: EMI 3C 053 00923M/EX 29 01633
CD: EMI CDH 769 7902
CD: Romophone 810152
CD: Fabbri GVS 21 |

GEORGES BIZET (1838–1875)

Carmen, excerpt (Je dis que rien ne m'épouvante)

New York 1918	Orchestra	Pathé (USA) 54031 Pathé (UK) 5361 LP: OASI 564 CD: Romophone 810102
New York March 1924	Orchestra Sodero	Edison 82324 LP: Esoteric (USA) 500 LP: Contrepoint (France) 20008 LP: Scala (USA) 849 LP: OASI 571 LP: Rubini RS 310 CD: Pearl GEMMCDS 9072 CD: Cantabile BIM 7052 CD: Romophone 810052

ARRIGO BOITO (1842–1918)

Mefistofele, excerpt (L'altra notte)

New York 1917	Orchestra	Pathé (USA) 63024 Pathé (Italy) 10347 LP: London International TWV 91053 LP: Scala (USA) 836 LP: OASI 566 LP: Rubini GV 576 CD: Romophone 810102 <u>TWV 91053 may contain the 1922 version</u>
New York March 1922	Orchestra Sodero	Edison 82305 LP: Esoteric (USA) 502 LP: Contrepoint (France) 20009 LP: OASI 571 LP: Belcantodisc BC 202 CD: Pearl GEMMCDS 9072 CD: Cantabile BIM 7052 CD: Romophone 810052
Milan June 1935	Orchestra Molajoli	78: Columbia LCX 25 78: Columbia (Italy) BQX 2504/BQX 2519 78: Columbia (Argentina) 266019 78: Columbia (USA) M 259/9168M LP: Columbia COLC 101 LP: Columbia (USA) ML 4404 LP: Angel 60111 LP: EMI 3C 053 00932M/EX 29 01633 CD: EMI CDH 769 7902 CD: Nimbus NI 7802/NI 7814/NI 7864 CD: Romophone 810152

GAETONO BRAGA (1829–1907)

La serenata

New York	Orchestra	Pathé (USA) 54024
1918	Sung in English	Pathé (France) 0333
		LP: OASI 526
		CD: Romophone 810102

HENRY BURLEIGH (1866–1949)

Jean

New York	Orchestra	Pathé 54067
1918		LP: OASI 526
		CD: Romophone 810102

ARTURO BUZZI-PECCIA (1854-1943)

Baciami!

New York 1918	Orchestra	Pathé (USA) 54057 Pathé (France) 0584 Pathé (Italy) 10350 Pathé (Spain) 6091 LP: OASI 526 CD: Romophone 810102

Colombetta

Milan April 1934	Orchestra Molajoli	78: Columbia (Italy) BQX 2501 78: Columbia (USA) 9084M LP: OASI 576 LP: Rubini CC 1 LP: Club 99 CL 501 LP: EMI EX 29 01633 CD: EMI CDH 769 7902 CD: Romophone 810152 CD: Fabbri GVS 21

Mal d'amore

New York February 1923	Unnamed pianist	Edison 82287
		LP: International Record Collectors
		    Club L 7008
		LP: OASI 526
		LP: Rubini RS 310
		LP: CBS Y 32676
		CD: Pearl GEMMCDS 9072
		CD: Cantabile BIM 7052
		CD: Minerva MNA 31
		CD: Romophone 810052
		CD: International Record Collectors
		    Club CD 801

ALFREDO CATALANI (1854–1893)

Loreley, excerpt (Dove son?)

New York April 1921	Orchestra Sodero	Edison unpublished
New York March 1922	Orchestra Sodero	Edison 82300 International Record Collectors Club 231 Bel Canto Club 1 LP: Esoteric (USA) 500 LP: Contrepoint (France) 20008 LP: Scala (USA) 849 LP: OASI 565 LP: Rubini RS 310 LP: Famous Records of the Past FRP 9 CD: Pearl GEMMCDS 9072 CD: Cantabile BIM 7052 CD: Memories HR 4475–4476 CD: Minerva MNA 31 CD: Romophone 810052

La Wally, excerpt (Ebben? Ne andrò lontana)

New York 1917	Orchestra	Pathé (USA) 63024 Pathé (Italy) 10420 LP: Scala (USA) 836 LP: OASI 577 LP: Top Artists' Platter 306 CD: Romophone 810102

New York
November
1920
	Orchestra
	Sodero
		Edison 82232/HRS 1061
		LP: International Record Collectors
		    Club L 7008
		LP: OASI 565
		LP: Rubini RS 310
		LP: CBS Y 33793
		CD: Pearl GEMMCDS 9072
		CD: Cantabile BIM 7052
		CD: Minerva MNA 31
		CD: Romophone 810052
		CD: International Record Collectors
		    Club CD 801

GUSTAVE CHARPENTIER (1860–1950)

Louise, excerpt (Depuis le jour)

New York   Orchestra   Pathé (USA) 54027
1918   Pathé (UK) 5590
                                     International Record Collectors Club 3134
                                     LP: Scala (USA) 836
                                     LP: OASI 566
                                     CD: Pearl GEMMCD 9143
                                     CD: Romophone 810102
                                     CD: International Record Collectors
                                         Club CD 801

FREDERIC CHOPIN (1810–1849)

Aspiration, arrangement of Nocturne in B

New York   Orchestra   Edison 82234
April 1921   Sodero   LP: OASI 526
                                     LP: CBS Y 33793
                                     LP: Rubini RS 310
                                     CD: Pearl GEMMCDS 9072
                                     CD: Cantabile BIM 7052
                                     CD: Minerva MNA 31
                                     CD: Romophone 810052

FRANCESCO CILEA (1866-1950)

Adriana Lecouvreur, excerpt (Io son l'umile ancella)

New York	Orchestra	Edison 82247/PRS 3
April 1921	Sodero	International Record Collectors Club 3071
		LP: Esoteric (USA) 508
		LP: Contrepoint (France) 20010
		LP: OASI 565
		LP: Scala (USA) 849
		LP: CBS Y 32676
		LP: Rubini GV 92/RS 310
		LP: EMI RLS 743
		CD: Pearl GEMMCDS 9072
		CD: Cantabile BIM 7052
		CD: Romophone 810052

Adriana Lecouvreur, excerpt (Poveri fiori)

Milan	Orchestra	78: Columbia LC 20
June 1935	Molajoli	78: Columbia (Italy) BQ 6001/BQ 6004
		78: Columbia (USA) 4134M
		LP: Columbia COLC 101
		LP: Angel 60111
		LP: EMI 3C 053 00932M/EX 29 01633
		CD: EMI CDH 769 7902
		CD: Romophone 810152
		CD: Fabbri GVS 21

L'Arlesiana, excerpt (Esser madre è un inferno)

Milan	Orchestra	78: Columbia LCX 28
June 1935	Molajoli	78: Columbia (Italy) BQX 2507
		78: Columbia (Argentina) 266019
		78: Columbia (USA) M 259/9168M
		LP: Columbia COLC 101
		LP: Columbia (USA) ML 4404
		LP: Angel 60111
		LP: EMI 3C 053 00903M/EX 29 01633
		CD: EMI CDH 769 7902
		CD: Romophone 810152
		CD: Fabbri GVS 21

BAINBRIDGE CRIST (1883–1969)

C'est mon ami

Milan	Orchestra	78: Columbia LCX 30
June 1935	Molajoli	78: Columbia (Italy) BQX 2509/BQX 2523
		78: Columbia (USA) M 289/9171M
		LP: OASI 577
		LP: EMI EX 29 01633
		CD: Romophone 810152

CLAUDE DEBUSSY (1862–1918)

Beau soir

Milan	Orchestra	78: Columbia LC 20
June 1935	Molajoli	78: Columbia (Italy) BQ 6001/BQ 6007
		78: Columbia (Argentina) 292543
		78: Columbia (USA) M 289/4398M
		LP: OASI 576
		LP: EMI EX 29 01633
		CD: Romophone 810152
		CD: Fabbri GVS 21

LEO DELIBES (1836–1891)

Bonjour Suzon!

New York 1918	Orchestra Sung in English	Pathé (USA) 54039 LP: OASI 566 LP: Rubini GV 576 CD: Pearl GEMMCD 9143 CD: Romophone 810102
Milan June 1935	Orchestra Molajoli	78: Columbia LC 19/LC 21 78: Columbia (Italy) BQ 6000/BQ 6007 78: Columbia (USA) M 289/4398M LP: OASI 576 LP: EMI EX 29 01633 CD: EMI CDH 769 7902 CD: Romophone 810152 CD: Fabbri GVS 21

Les filles de Cadiz

Milan June 1935	Orchestra Molajoli	78: Columbia LCX 29 78: Columbia (Italy) BQX 2508/BQX 2523 78: Columbia (USA) M 289/9171M LP: OASI 577 LP: EMI EX 29 01633 CD: EMI CDH 769 7902 CD: Romophone 810152

STEFANO DONAUDY (1879-1925)

O del mio amato ben

New York April 1922	Orchestra Sodero	Edison unpublished CD: Pearl GEMMCDS 9072 CD: Romophone 810102
Milan June 1935	Orchestra Molajoli	78: Columbia LX 635/LCX 25 78: Columbia (Italy) BQX 2504/BQX 2524 78: Columbia (USA) 9112M/9169M LP: OASI 576 LP: EMI EX 29 01633 CD: EMI CDH 769 7902 CD: Nimbus NI 7802 CD: Romophone 810152

Spirate pur

Milan June 1935	Orchestra Molajoli	78: Columbia LC 21 78: Columbia (Italy) BQ 6002/BQ 6005 78: Columbia (USA) 4135M/4397M LP: OASI 577 LP: EMI EX 29 01633 CD: EMI CDH 769 7902 CD: Romophone 810152

UMBERTO GIORDANO (1867-1948)

Andrea Chenier, excerpt (La mamma morta)

New York November 1920	Orchestra Sodero	Edison 82224 LP: Esoteric (USA) 508 LP: Contrepoint (France) 20010 LP: OASI 571 LP: CBS Y 33793 LP: Rubini RS 310 CD: Pearl GEMMCDS 9072 CD: Cantabile BIM 7052 CD: Romophone 810052
Milan June 1935	Orchestra Molajoli	78: Columbia LX 655/LCX 28/LCX 102 78: Columbia (Italy) BQX 2507 78: Columbia (Argentina) 264842 78: Columbia (USA) M 259 LP: Columbia COLC 101 LP: Columbia (USA) ML 4404 LP: Angel 60111 LP: EMI 3C 053 00932M/EX 29 01633 CD: EMI CDH 769 7902 CD: Romophone 810152

Madame Sans-Gêne, excerpt (Che me ne faccio del vostro castello)

New York 1917	Orchestra	Pathé (USA) 63023 LP: London International TWV 91053 LP: OASI 566 CD: Romophone 810102 TWV 91053 may contain the 1922 version
New York March 1922	Orchestra Sodero	Edison 82305 International Record Collectors Club 3083 LP: Esoteric (USA) 502 LP: Contrepoint (France) 20009 LP: OASI 565 LP: Belcantodisc BC 202 LP: Rubini RS 310 CD: Pearl GEMMCDS 9072 CD: Cantabile BIM 7052 CD: Romophone 810052 CD: Fabbri GVS 21

Canzone guerresca

New York 1917	Orchestra	Pathé (USA) 63020/CRS 56 Pathé (Italy) 10348 LP: OASI 526 CD: Pearl GEMMCD 9143 CD: Romophone 810102

CHRISTOPH WILLIBALD GLUCK (1714–1787)

Paride ed Elena, excerpt (Spiagge amati)

New York	Unnamed pianist	Edison 82287
February		International Record Collectors Club 192
1923		LP: Esoteric (USA) 508
		LP: Contrepoint (France) 20010
		LP: Scala (USA) 849
		LP: OASI 571
		LP: Rubini RS 310
		LP: CBS Y 32676
		CD: Pearl GEMMCDS 9072
		CD: Cantabile BIM 7052
		CD: Minerva MNA 31
		CD: Romophone 810052

CARLOS GOMES (1836–1896)

Salvator Rosa, excerpt (Mia piccirella)

New York	Orchestra	Edison 82216
November	Sodero	LP: International Record Collectors
1920		Club L 7008
		LP: OASI 565
		LP: Rubini RS 310
		LP: CBS Y 33793
		CD: Pearl GEMMCDS 9072
		CD: Cantabile BIM 7052
		CD: Romophone 810052
		CD: International Record Collectors
		Club CD 801

GUAGNI-BENVENUTI

Guardami!

New York	Orchestra	Edison 82339
March 1924	Sodero	LP: OASI 577
		LP: Rubini RS 310
		CD: Pearl GEMMCDS 9072
		CD: Cantabile BIM 7052
		CD: Minerva MNA 31
		CD: Romophone 810052

GEORGE FRIDERIC HANDEL (1685-1759)

Rinaldo, excerpt (Lascia ch' io pianga!)

New York	Orchestra	Edison 82300
April 1922	Sodero	LP: Esoteric (USA) 500
		LP: Contrepoint (France) 20008
		LP: Scala (USA) 849
		LP: OASI 577
		LP: Rubini RS 310
		LP: CBS Y 32676
		CD: Pearl GEMMCDS 9072
		CD: Cantabile BIM 7052
		CD: Minerva MNA 31
		CD: Romophone 810052

VICTOR HERBERT (1859-1924)

Orange Blossoms, excerpt (A kiss in the dark)

New York	Orchestra	Edison 82317
March 1924	Sodero	LP: International Record Collectors
		Club L 7008
		LP: OASI 526
		LP: Rubini RS 310
		CD: Pearl GEMMCDS 9072
		CD: Cantabile BIM 7052
		CD: Romophone 810052
		CD: International Record Collectors
		Club CD 801

EDISON
RECORD

A PRODUCT OF
THE EDISON
LABORATORIES

82300-R
FIGLIO DEL SOL, MIO DOLCE
AMOR
FROM "L'AFRICANA"
(Meyerbeer)
Soprano in Italian
CLAUDIA MUZIO
PRICE $2.00 in the U.S.A.

EDISON
RECORD

A PRODUCT OF
THE EDISON
LABORATORIES

82300-L
LASCIA CH'IO PIANGA
FROM "RINALDO"
(Handel)
Soprano in Italian
CLAUDIA MUZIO
PRICE $2.00 in the U.S.A.

CLAUDIA **MUZIO** SINGS

ERNANI (Verdi):
Ernani involami

TOSCA (Puccini):
Vissi d'arte

TROVATORE (Verdi):
D'amor sull' ali rosee

LOUISE (Charpentier):
Depuis le jour

BOHEME (Puccini):
Mi chiamano Mimi
Musetta's Waltz

WALLY (Catalani):
Ebben, ne andro lontano

CAVALLERIA RUSTICANA (Mascagni):
Voi lo sapete

PAGLIACCI (Leoncavallo):
Ballatella

WILLIAM TELL (Rossini):
Romance

MASKED BALL (Verdi):
Ma dall' arido

MANON LESCAUT (Puccini):
In quelle trine

AIDA (Verdi):
O patria mia

OTELLO (Verdi):
Ave Maria

MADAMA BUTTERFLY (Puccini):
Entrance of Butterfly

MEFISTOFELE (Boito):
L'altra notte

SCALA 836

RUGGERO LEONCAVALLO (1858–1919)

I pagliacci, excerpt (Qual fiamma avea nel guardo/Stridono lassù)

New York 1917	Orchestra	Pathé (USA) 63017 Pathé (Italy) 10346 LP: London International TWV 91053 LP: Scala (USA) 836 LP: OASI 568 CD: Pearl GEMMCD 9143 CD: Romophone 810102
New York October 1920	Orchestra Sodero	Edison unpublished
New York January 1921	Orchestra Sodero	Edison 82232 International Record Collectors Club 175 LP: Esoteric (USA) 502 LP: Contrepointe (France) 20009 LP: OASI 565 LP: Belcantodisc BC 202 LP: Rubini RS 310 LP: CBS Y 33793 CD: Pearl GEMMCDS 9072 CD: Cantabile BIM 7052 CD: Romophone 810052

I pagliacci, excerpt (Nedda! Silvio! A quest' ora?)

New York	Laurenti	Edison 82247
March 1921	Orchestra	International Record Collectors Club 3071
	Sodero	LP: London International TWV 91053
		LP: Esoteric (USA) 502
		LP: Contrepoint (France) 20009
		LP: Belcantodisc BC 202
		LP: Rubini GV 92/RS 310
		LP: OASI 565
		LP: CBS Y 32676
		CD: Pearl GEMMCDS 9072
		CD: Cantabile BIM 7052
		CD: Romophone 810052

Zaza, excerpt (Ammogliato/Dir che ci sono al mondo)

New York	Orchestra	Edison unpublished
November	Sodero	
1920		
New York	Piano and string	Edison 82243/PRS 3
March 1921	accompaniment	International Record Collectors Club 3135
		LP: OASI 565
		LP: Scala (USA) 849
		LP: Rubini RS 310
		LP: CBS Y 32676
		CD: Pearl GEMMCDS 9072
		CD: Cantabile BIM 7052
		CD: Minerva MNA 31
		CD: Romophone 810052
		CD: Fabbri GVS 21
		Pearl incorrectly states accompaniment to
		be orchestra conducted by Sodero

PIETRO MASCAGNI (1863-1945)

L'amico Fritz, excerpt (Son pochi fiori)

New York	Unnamed pianist	Edison 82291
February		International Record Collectors Club 3083
1923		LP: OASI 571
		LP: Scala (USA) 849
		LP: Rubini RS 310
		LP: CBS Y 32676
		CD: Pearl GEMMCDS 9072
		CD: Cantabile BIM 7052
		CD: Romophone 810052

Cavalleria rusticana, excerpt (Voi lo sapete)

New York	Orchestra	Pathé (USA) 54021
1918		Pathé (UK) 5699
		Pathé (Italy) 10436
		LP: OASI 566
		LP: Scala (USA) 836
		CD: Romophone 810102
Milan	Orchestra	78: Columbia LX 583/LCX 20
April 1934	Molajoli	78: Columbia (Italy) BQX 2501
		78: Columbia (Argentina) 264955
		78: Columbia (USA) 9084M
		LP: Columbia COLC 101
		LP: Angel 60111
		LP: EMI 3C 053 0932M/EX 29 01633
		CD: EMI CDH 769 7902
		CD: Romophone 810152
		CD: Fabbri GVS 21

ANGELO MASCHERONI (1855-1905)

Eternamente

New York November 1920	Orchestra Spalding, violin Sung in English	Edison unpublished LP: CBS Y 33793 CD: Romophone 810102
New York April 1921	Spalding, violin Gaylor, piano	Edison 82243 LP: Esoteric (USA) 508 LP: Contrepoint (France) 20010 LP: OASI 526 LP: Rubini RS 310 CD: Pearl GEMMCDS 9072 CD: Cantabile BIM 7052 CD: Minerva MNA 31 CD: Romophone 810052

VICTOR MASSE (1822-1884)

Paul et Virginie, excerpt (Parmi les lianes)

New York March 1924	Orchestra Sodero	Edison unpublished

JULES MASSENET (1842–1912)

Hérodiade, excerpt (Il est doux, il est bon)

New York	Orchestra	Edison 82309
April 1922	Sodero	LP: Esoteric (USA) 500
	Sung in Italian	LP: Contrepoint (France) 20008
		LP: OASI 571
		LP: Scala (USA) 849
		LP: Rubini RS 310
		CD: Pearl GEMMCDS 9072
		CD: Cantabile BIM 7052
		CD: Minerva MNA 31
		CD: Romophone 810052

Manon, excerpt (Obéissons, quand leur voix appelle)

New York	Orchestra	Pathé (USA) 54030
1918		Pathé (UK) 5361
		LP: OASI 564
		CD: Pearl GEMMCD 9143
		CD: Romophone 810102

GIACOMO MEYERBEER (1791–1864)

L'Africaine, excerpt (Sur mes genoux)

New York	Orchestra	Edison 82300
April 1922	Sodero	LP: Esoteric (USA) 500
	Sung in Italian	LP: Contrepoint (France) 20008
		LP: OASI 577
		LP: Scala (USA) 849
		LP: Rubini RS 310
		CD: Pearl GEMMCDS 9072
		CD: Cantabile BIM 7052
		CD: Minerva MNA 31
		CD: Romophone 810052

GORDON MONAHAN

Shepherd's love

New York March 1924	Orchestra Sodero	Edison 82317 LP: OASI 526 LP: Rubini RS 310 CD: Pearl GEMMCDS 9072 CD: Cantabile BIM 7052 CD: Minerva MNA 31 CD: Romophone 810052

JACQUES OFFENBACH (1819-1880)

Les contes D'Hoffmann, excerpt (Belle nuit, o nuit d'amour)

New York 1918	Orchestra Howard, mezzo-sop	Pathé (USA) 54026 Pathé (France) 0333 LP: OASI 566 LP: Rubini RS 310 CD: Cantabile BIM 7052 CD: Romophone 810102

Les contes d'Hoffmann, excerpt (Elle a fui, la tourterelle)

New York March 1924	Orchestra Sodero	Edison 82324 LP: Esoteric (USA) 508 LP: Contrepoint (France) 20010 LP: OASI 571 CD: Pearl GEMMCDS 9072 CD: Romophone 810052

OLIVIER-MERCANTINI

Inno di Garibaldi

New York 1917	Orchestra	Pathé (USA) 63020/CRS 56 Pathé (Italy) 10348 LP: OASI 526 LP: Top Artists' Platter 315 CD: Romophone 810102

ALESSANDRO PARISOTTI (1835–1913)

Se tu m'ami, previously attributed to Ciampi and Pergolesi

Orange NJ January 1925	Orchestra	Edison 82339 LP: Esoteric (USA) 508 LP: Contrepoint (France) 20010 LP: OASI 577 CD: Pearl GEMMCD 9143 CD: Romophone 810052
Milan June 1935	Orchestra Molajoli	78: Columbia LX 635/LCX 26 78: Columbia (Italy) BQX 2505/BQX 2524 78: Columbia (USA) M 289/9169M LP: OASI 576 LP: Rubini RS 310 LP: EMI EX 29 01633 CD: EMI CDH 769 7902 CD: Cantabile BIM 7052 CD: Minerva MNA 31 CD: Romophone 810152 CD: Fabbri GVS 21

AMILCARE PONCHIELLI (1834–1886)

La Gioconda, excerpt (Suicidio!)

New York 1917	Orchestra	Pathé (USA) 63019 LP: OASI 568 CD: Pearl GEMMCD 9143 CD: Romophone 810102

GIACOMO PUCCINI (1858–1924)

La Bohème, excerpt (Si mi chiamano Mimì)

Milan June 1911	Orchestra	Gramophone Company 053264/AGSB 14 Victor 55028 International Record Collectors Club 39 LP: Victor LCT 6701 LP: HMV CSLP 501 CD: Pearl GEMMCDS 9925 CD: Nimbus NI 7814 CD: Romophone 810052 CD: Fabbri GVS 21
New York June 1914	Orchestra	Edison unpublished
New York 1917	Orchestra	Pathé (USA) 63022 Pathé (UK) 5173 Pathé (France) 0330 LP: OASI 526/OASI 568 LP: Scala (USA) 836 CD: Romophone 810102
Orange NJ January 1921	Orchestra Sodero	Edison 82234 LP: OASI 571 LP: Rubini RS 310 LP: CBS Y 33793 CD: Pearl GEMMCD 9143 CD: Cantabile BIM 7052 CD: Romophone 810052
Milan June 1935	Orchestra Molajoli	78: Columbia LX 583/LCX 29 78: Columbia (Italy) BQX 2508/BQX 2519 78: Columbia (USA) M 257 LP: Columbia COLC 101 LP: Columbia (USA) ML 4404 LP: HMV CSLP 501 LP: Angel 60111 LP: EMI 3C 053 00932M/EX 29 01633 CD: EMI CDH 769 7902 CD: Romophone 810152

Claudia Muzio

the
complete
HMV
(1911)
and Edison
(1920~25)
recordings

Claudia Muzio

the
complete
Pathé
recordings
(1917~18)

La Bohème, excerpt (Donde lieta usci)

Milan June 1911	Orchestra	Gramophone Company unpublished
Milan June 1935	Orchestra Molajoli	78: Columbia LB 40/LC 22/LC 31 78: Columbia (Italy) BQ 6003/BQ 6006 78: Columbia (Argentina) 292507 78: Columbia (USA) 4140M LP: Columbia COLC 101 LP: Angel 60111 LP: EMI EX 29 01633 CD: EMI CDH 769 7902 CD: Romophone 810152

La Bohème, excerpt (O soave fanciulla)

Milan June 1911	Orchestra Unnamed tenor	Gramophone Company unpublished

La Bohème, excerpt (Quando m'en vo)

New York 1918	Orchestra	Pathé (USA) 54050 Pathé (UK) 5452 Pathé (France) 0584 Pathé (Italy) 10350 LP: OASI 564 LP: Scala (USA) 836 CD: Pearl GEMMCD 9143 CD: Romophone 810102

Gianni Schicchi, excerpt (O mio babbino caro)

New York 1918	Orchestra	Pathé (USA) 54042 Pathé (Italy) 10531 Actuelle 025106 LP: OASI 564 CD: Pearl GEMMCD 9143 CD: Romophone 810102

Madama Butterfly, excerpt (Un bel dì)

New York   Orchestra   Pathé (USA) 54016
1918   Pathé (UK) 5404
                                     Pathé (Italy) 10420
                                     LP: OASI 566
                                     CD: Romophone 810102

Madama Butterfly, excerpt (Ancora un passo or via)

New York   Orchestra   Pathé (USA) 63022
1917   Chorus   Pathé (UK) 5173
                                     Pathé (France) 0330/0581
                                     Pathé (Italy) 10344
                                     Actuelle 025072
                                     Perfect 11511
                                     LP: London International TWV 91053
                                     LP: Esoteric (USA) 502
                                     LP: Contrepoint (France) 20009
                                     LP: Scala (USA) 836
                                     LP: Belcantodisc BC 202
                                     LP: OASI 568
                                     LP: Rubini GV 576
                                     CD: Pearl GEMMCD 9143
                                     CD: Romophone 810102

Manon Lescaut, excerpt (In quelle trine morbide)

New York   Orchestra   Pathé (USA) 63017
1917   Pathé (UK) 5608
                                     Pathé (Italy) 10418
                                     Actuelle 025109
                                     International Record Collectors Club 3135
                                     LP: OASI 568
                                     LP: Scala (USA) 836
                                     LP: Rubini GV 576
                                     CD: Pearl GEMMCD 9143
                                     CD: Romophone 810102

New York   Orchestra   Pathé 67203
1918

Suor Angelica, excerpt (Senza mamma)

New York 1918	Orchestra	Pathé (USA) 54036 Pathé (Italy) 10351 LP: OASI 564 LP: Rubini GV 576 CD: Pearl GEMMCD 9143 CD: Romophone 810102

Tosca, excerpt (Vissi d'arte)

New York 1917	Orchestra	Pathé (USA) 63018 Pathé (UK) 5174 Actuelle 025087 Davega 8010 LP: London International TWV 91053 LP: Esoteric (USA) 502 LP: Contrepoint (France) 20009 LP: Scala (USA) 836 LP: OASI 564 LP: Top Artists' Platter 308 LP: Belcantodisc BC 202 LP: Rubini GV 576 CD: Pearl GEMMCD 9143 CD: Romophone 810102
Milan June 1935	Orchestra Molajoli	78: Columbia LB 40/LC 19 78: Columbia (Italy) BQ 6000/BQ 6006 78: Columbia (Argentina) 292507 78: Columbia (USA) 4140M LP: Columbia COLC 101 LP: Angel 60111 LP: EMI 3C 053 00932M/EX 29 01633 CD: EMI CDH 769 7902 CD: Nimbus NI 7814 CD: Romophone 810152 CD: Fabbri GVS 21

Tosca, extract (Gente là dentro!...to end of Act 1)

San Francisco October 1932	Borgioli, Windheim, Gandolfi, D'Angelo, Argall San Francisco SO and Opera Chorus Merola	LP: Ed Smith EJS 129 LP: Collectors' Limited Edition MDP 028 LP: Edizione lirica EL 002 CD: Romophone 810152 CD: Eklipse EKR 48

LICINIO REFICE (1885-1954)

Cecilia, excerpt (Per amor di Gesù)

Milan	Orchestra	78: Columbia LX 19
April 1934	Refice	78: Columbia (Italy) BQX 2500
		78: Columbia (USA) X 112/9089M/9148M
		LP: Ed Smith EJS 312
		LP: OASI 576
		LP: EMI EX 20 01633
		CD: Romophone 810152
		CD: Fabbri GVS 21

Cecilia, excerpt (Grazie, sorella!)

Milan	Orchestra	78: Columbia LX 24
June 1935	Refice	78: Columbia (Italy) BQX 2503
		78: Columbia (USA) X 112
		LP: Ed Smith EJS 312
		LP: OASI 576
		LP: EMI EX 29 01633
		CD: Romophone 810152
		CD: Fabbri GVS 21

Ave Maria

Milan	Orchestra	78: Columbia LCX 27
June 1935	Refice	78: Columbia (Italy) BQX 2506/BQX 2521
		78: Columbia (USA) M 289/9170M
		LP: OASI 576
		LP: EMI EX 29 01633
		CD: Romophone 810152

Ombra di nube

Milan	Orchestra	78: Columbia LCX 23
June 1935	Refice	78: Columbia (Italy) BQX 2502/BQX 2521
		78: Columbia (USA) M 289/9170M
		LP: OASI 576
		LP: EMI EX 29 01633
		CD: EMI CDH 769 7902
		CD: Nimbus NI 7801
		CD: Romophone 810152

MAX REGER (1873-1916)

Mariae Wiegenlied

Milan	Orchestra	78: Columbia LC 22
June 1935	Molajoli	78: Columbia (Italy) BQ 6003/BQ 6005
	Sung in Italian	78: Columbia (USA) 4135M/4397M
		LP: OASI 576
		LP: EMI EX 29 01633
		CD: Romophone 810152
		CD: RCA/BMG 75605 522822

GIOACHINO ROSSINI (1792-1868)

Guilleaume Tell, excerpt (Sombres forêts)

New York	Orchestra	Pathé (USA) 54025
1918	Sung in Italian	Pathé (Italy) 10346
		Actuelle 025104
		LP: London International TWV 91053
		LP: Esoteric (USA) 502
		LP: Contrepoint (France) 20009
		LP: OASI 564
		LP: Scala (USA) 836
		LP: Belcantodisc BC 202
		CD: Pearl GEMMCD 9143
		CD: Romophone 810102

La separazione

New York	Unnamed pianist	Edison 82291
February		LP: Esoteric (USA) 508
1923		LP: Contrepoint (France) 20010
		LP: OASI 526
		LP: CBS Y 32676
		LP: Rubini RS 310
		CD: Pearl GEMMCDS 9072
		CD: Cantabile BIM 7052
		CD: Minerva MNA 31
		CD: Romophone 810052

EMANUELE DE ROXAS (1827-1891)

O ben tornato, amore!

New York 1918	Orchestra	Pathé (USA) 54062 Pathé (Spain) 6091 LP: OASI 566 CD: Romophone 810102

WILFRED SANDERSON (1878-1935)

Until

New York 1918	Orchestra	Pathé (USA) 54038 LP: OASI 526 CD: Romophone 810102

CESARE SODERO (1886-1947)

Crisantemi

New York November 1920	Orchestra Sodero	Edison 82218 LP: OASI 526 LP: Rubini RS 310 LP: CBS Y 33793 CD: Pearl GEMMCDS 9072 CD: Cantabile BIM 7052 CD: Romophone 810052

PIOTR TCHAIKOVSKY (1840-1893)

Evgeny Onegin, excerpt (Tatiana's Letter scene)

New York	Orchestra	Edison 82224/HRS 1061
November	Sodero	LP: Esoteric (USA) 500
1920	Sung in Italian	LP: Contrepoint (France) 20008
		LP: OASI 565
		LP: Scala (USA) 849
		LP: Mark 56 Records 723
		LP: Rubini RS 310
		LP: CBS Y 33793
		CD: Pearl GEMMCDS 9072
		CD: Cantabile BIM 7052
		CD: Minerva MNA 31
		CD: Romophone 810052

AMBROISE THOMAS (1811-1896)

Mignon, excerpt (Connais-tu le pays?)

New York	Orchestra	Pathé (USA) 63023
1917	Sung in Italian	Pathé (UK) 5590
		Pathé (France) 0581
		Pathé (Italy) 10344
		LP: OASI 568
		CD: Pearl GEMMCDS 9143
		CD: Romophone 810102

GIUSEPPE VERDI (1813-1901)

Aida, excerpt (Ritorna vincitor!)

New York 1917	Orchestra	Pathé (USA) 63021 Pathé (UK) 5644 Pathé (France) 0329 Pathé (Italy) 10345 International Record Collectors Club 3003 LP: OASI 568/OASI 577 LP: Rubini GV 576 CD: Pearl GEMMCD 9143 CD: Romophone 810102 <u>Pathé UK and Italian issues contained only</u> <u>first part of aria (up to I sacri nomi)</u>

Aida, excerpt (O patria mia)

New York 1918	Orchestra	Pathé (USA) 54015 Pathé (UK) 5644 Pathé (Italy) 10345 Actuelle 025106 International Record Collectors Club 3019 LP: OASI 568 LP: Scala (USA) 836 LP: Rubini GV 576 CD: Pearl GEMMCD 9143 CD: Romophone 810102

Un ballo in maschera, excerpt (Ma dall' arido stelo divulsa)

New York 1918	Orchestra	Pathé (USA) 54036 Pathé (France) 0583 Pathé (Italy) 10349 Actuelle 025104 Perfect 11540 LP: OASI 568 LP: Scala (USA) 836 LP: Rubini GV 576 CD: Pearl GEMMCD 9143 CD: Romophone 810102

Ernani, excerpt (Surta è la notte/Ernani, involami!)

New York 1918	Orchestra	Pathé (USA) 54053 Pathé (UK) 5452 Actuelle 025072 Perfect 11511 LP: London International TWV 91053 LP: Esoteric (USA) 502 LP: Contrepoint (France) 20009 LP: OASI 564 LP: Scala (USA) 836 LP: Belcantodisc BC 202 LP: Rubini GV 576 CD: Romophone 810102

La forza del destino, excerpt (Pace, pace, mio Dio!)

New York 1917	Orchestra	Pathé (USA) 63025 Pathé (UK) 5377 CD: Romophone 810102
New York March 1922	Orchestra Sodero	Edison 82267 LP: Esoteric (USA) 508 LP: Contrepoint (France) 20010 LP: OASI 571 LP: Rubini RS 310 LP: CBS Y 32676 CD: Pearl GEMMCDS 9072 CD: Cantabile BIM 7052 CD: Romophone 810052
Milan June 1935	Orchestra Molajoli	78: Columbia LX 622/LCX 26/LCX 102 78: Columbia (Italy) BQX 2505/BQX 2520 78: Columbia (Argentina) 264960 78: Columbia (USA) M 259/9166M LP: Columbia COLC 101 LP: Columbia (USA) ML 4404 LP: Angel 60111 LP: EMI 3C 053 00932M/EX 29 01633 CD: Romophone 810152 CD: Fabbri GVS 21

I Lombardi, excerpt (O madre dal cielo soccorri al mio pianto!)

New York	Orchestra	Edison 82309
May 1922	Sodero	International Record Collectors Club 175
		LP: Esoteric (USA) 500
		LP: Contrepoint (France) 20008
		LP: OASI 565
		LP: Scala (USA) 849
		LP: Top Artists' Platter 314
		LP: Rubini RS 310
		CD: Pearl GEMMCDS 9072
		CD: Cantabile BIM 7052
		CD: Minerva MNA 31
		CD: Romophone 810052

Otello, excerpt (Ave Maria)

New York	Orchestra	Pathé 63019
1917		International Record Collectors Club 3019
		LP: OASI 568
		LP: Scala (USA) 836
		CD: Pearl GEMMCD 9143
		CD: Romophone 810102

Otello, excerpt (Già nella notte densa)

Milan	Merli	78: Columbia LX 550/LCX 31/LCX 149
June 1935	Orchestra	78: Columbia (Italy) BQX 2510
	Molajoli	78: Columbia (France) LFX 466
		78: Columbia (Argentina) 264617
		78: Columbia (USA) 9100M
		LP: Columbia (USA) ML 4404
		LP: EMI 3C 053 17660M/EX 29 01633
		CD: ASV Living Era AJA 5177
		CD: Preiser 89091
		CD: Romophone 810152

Muzio's part in this recording was also spliced into Martinelli's recording of the tenor part (from his 1939 version with Jepson on Victor M 620) to form a composite version of the duet which was issued on Ed Smith LP EJS 270

Otello, excerpt (Dio ti giocondi!)

Milan	Merli	78: Columbia LX 551/LCX 32/LCX 150
June 1935	Orchestra	78: Columbia (Italy) BQX 2511
	Molajoli	78: Columbia (France) LFX 467
		78: Columbia (Germany) LWX 159
		78: Columbia (USA) 9102M
		LP: Columbia (USA) ML 4404
		LP: EMI 3C 053 17660M/EX 29 01633
		CD: Preiser 89091
		CD: Romophone 810152

La traviata, excerpt (Che gli dirò/Amami Alfredo!)

Milan	Tommasini	Gramophone Company 254063
1911	Orchestra	LP: OASI 526
		CD: Romophone 810052

La traviata, excerpt (Addio del passato)

New York	Orchestra	Pathé (USA) 54022
1918		Pathé (UK) 5404
		Pathé (Italy) 10347
		LP: OASI 566
		CD: Romophone 810102
		This version begins at Attendo, attendo!
Milan	Orchestra	78: Columbia LX 655/LCX 30
June 1935	Molajoli	78: Columbia (Italy) BQX 2509/BQX 2522
		78: Columbia (Argentina) 264842
		78: Columbia (USA) M 259/9166M
		LP: Columbia COLC 101
		LP: Columbia (USA) ML 4404
		LP: Angel 60111
		LP: EMI 3C 053 00932M/EX 29 01633/
		EX 29 10753
		CD: EMI CDH 769 7902
		CD: Iron Needle IN 1304
		CD: Romophone 810152
		CD: Fabbri GVS 21
		This version begins at Teneste la promessa

Il trovatore, excerpt (Tacea la notte placida)

New York 1917	Orchestra	Pathé (USA) 63018 Pathé (UK) 5174 Pathé (Italy) 10436 Actuelle 025072 LP: OASI 564 LP: Rubini GV 576 CD: Pearl GEMMCD 9143 CD: Romophone 810102
New York November 1920	Orchestra Sodero	Edison 82223 LP: Esoteric (USA) 508 LP: Contrepoint (France) 20010 LP: OASI 571 LP: Rubini RS 310 LP: CBS Y 33793 CD: Pearl GEMMCDS 9072 CD: Cantabile BIM 7052 CD: Romophone 810052
Milan June 1935	Orchestra Molajoli	78: Columbia LC 21/LC 31 78: Columbia (Italy) BQ 6002/BQ 6004 78: Columbia (USA) 4134M LP: Columbia COLC 101 LP: Angel 60111 LP: EMI 3C 053 00932M/EX 29 01633 CD: EMI CDH 769 7902/CHS 764 8642 CD: Romophone 810152 CD: Fabbri GVS 21

Il trovatore, excerpt (Di tale amor)

Milan 1911	Orchestra	Gramophone Company unpublished
New York November 1920	Orchestra Sodero	Edison 82223 LP: Esoteric (USA) 508 LP: Contrepoint (France) 20010 LP: OASI 571 LP: Rubini RS 310 LP: CBS Y 33793 CD: Pearl GEMMCDS 9072 CD: Cantabile BIM 7052 CD: Romophone 810052

Il trovatore, excerpt (D'amor sull' ali rosee)

New York 1918	Orchestra	Pathé (USA) 54029 Pathé (UK) 5068 Pathé (France) 0583 Pathé (Italy) 10439 Actuelle 025087 Perfect 10375 LP: London International TWV 91053 LP: OASI 566 LP: Scala (USA) 836 LP: Rubini GV 576 CD: Pearl GEMMCD 9143 CD: Romophone 810102 TWV 91053 may contain the December 1920 version
New York November 1920	Orchestra Sodero	Edison unpublished
New York December 1920	Orchestra Sodero	Edison 82223 LP: Esoteric (USA) 502 LP: Contrepoint (France) 20009 LP: OASI 571 LP: Belcantodisc BC 202 LP: Rubini RS 310 LP: CBS Y 33793 CD: Pearl GEMMCDS 9072 CD: Cantabile BIM 7052 CD: Romophone 810052

I vespri siciliani, excerpt (Mercè dilette amiche!)

New York 1918	Orchestra	Pathé (USA) 54044 Pathé (UK) 5699 Pathé (Italy) 10352 LP: OASI 564 CD: Romophone 810102
New York March 1924	Orchestra Sodero	Edison 82300 International Record Collectors Club 231 Bel Canto Club 1 LP: Esoteric (USA) 500 LP: Contrepoint (France) 20008 LP: OASI 571 LP: Scala (USA) 849 LP: Rubini RS 310 CD: Pearl GEMMCDS 9072 CD: Cantabile BIM 7052 CD: Romophone 810052

ERMANNO WOLF-FERRARI (1876-1948)

Il segreto di Susanna, excerpt (O gioia la nube leggera!)

New York	Orchestra	Pathé (USA) 63025
1917		Pathé (UK) 5377
		International Record Collectors Club 3134
		LP: OASI 564
		CD: Pearl GEMMCD 9143
		CD: Romophone 810102

MISCELLANEOUS
Composers unknown

Il pescatore canta

New York	Edison unpublished
March 1924	

Mon jardin

New York	Orchestra	Edison unpublished
January	Sodero	CD: Pearl GEMMCDS 9072
1925		CD: Romophone 810102

Odorano le rose

New York	Orchestra	Edison unpublished
April 1922	Sodero	LP: Ed Smith UORC 341
		LP: Rubini GV 105/RS 310
		CD: Pearl GEMMCDS 9072
		CD: Cantabile BIM 7052
		CD: Romophone 810052

Torna amore!

New York	Orchestra	Edison unpublished
March 1924	Sodero	CD: Pearl GEMMCDS 9072
		CD: Romophone 810102

Maria Callas
1923 -1977

Discography compiled
by John Hunt

LUDWIG VAN BEETHOVEN (1770-1827)

Ah perfido!, concert aria

Paris
December
1963–
January
1964
	Conservatoire
	Orchestra
	Rescigno
		LP: Columbia 33CX 1990/SAX 2540
		LP: Columbia (Germany) C 91359/STC 91359
		LP: Angel 36200
		LP: World Records T 690/ST 690
		LP: EMI 1C 053 01360/2C 069 01360/
		    3C 065 01360/2C165 54178-54188
		CD: EMI CDC 754 4372/CDS 749 4532/
		    CMS 763 6252/CMS 565 5342/
		    CZS 252 6142

Paris March 1976	Tate, piano	CD: Eklipse EKR 14 CD: Gala GL 320 <u>Recording incomplete and incorrectly</u> <u>described by Eklipse as being</u> <u>accompanied by the singer herself</u>

VINCENZO BELLINI (1801-1835)

Norma

Mexico City
May 1950
	Role of Norma
	De lo Santos,
	Simionato, Baum,
	Moscona
	Bellas Artes
	Orchestra & Chorus
	Picco
		LP: Historical Recording Enterprises
		    HRE 252
		CD: Melodram MEL 26018
		Excerpts
		LP: Opus 91
		LP: Historical Recording Enterprises
		    HRE 219
		CD: Rodolphe RPC 32484-32487

London November 1952	Sutherland, Stignani, Picchi, Vaghi Covent Garden Orchestra & Chorus Gui	LP: BJR Records OMY 200/BJR 155 LP: MRF Records MRF 11 LP: Collectors Limited Editions ARPCL 32014 CD: Legato LCD 130 CD: Melodram MEL 26025 CD: Verona 27018 -27020
Trieste November 1953	Ronchini, Nicolai, Corelli, Christoff Teatro Verdi Orchestra & Chorus Votto	LP: Historical Recording Enterprises HRE 283 CD: Melodram 26031 HRE 283 was an abridged version Excerpts CD: Myto MCD 91340

Milan
April-May
1954
	Cavallari,
	Stignani,
	Filippeschi,
	Rossi-Lemeni
	La Scala
	Orchestra & Chorus
	Serafin
		LP: Columbia 33CX 1179-1181
		LP: Columbia (Germany) C 90377-90379
		LP: Angel 3517/6037
		LP: EMI 2C 163 00944-00946/
		    2C163 03565-03567/2C163 52780-52787/
		    3C163 00944-00946/SLS 5115/
		    EX 29 00663
		CD: EMI CDS 747 3048/CDS 556 2712/
		    CMS 252 9432
		Excerpts
		45: Columbia SEL 1536/SEL 1550/SEL 1586
		LP: Columbia (France) FCX 30312
		LP: Angel 35379
		LP: EMI 1C 061 00741/1C 053 01017M/
		    1C 191 01593-01594M/3C 063 00741/
		    3C 063 01017/SLS 5057/SLS 5104
		CD: EMI CDS 749 6002/CDS 754 1032/
		    CMS 763 2442/CMS 764 4182/
		    CMS 565 5342/CZS 252 1642

Norma/continued

Rome June 1955	Cavallari, Stigani, Del Monaco, Modesti RAI Roma Orchestra & Chorus Serafin	LP: Opera viva JLT 6 LP: Discophilia KS 22-24 LP: Cetra LAR 28 LP: Replica RPL 2416-2418 LP: Melodram MEL 017 LP: Movimento musica 03.005 CD: Cetra CDC 4 CD: Hunt CDLSMH 34029/CDMP 429 CD: Movimento musica 013.014 CD: Virtuoso 269.9062 Excerpts LP: Gioielli della lirica GML 03 CD: Foyer CDS 15002 CD: Di Stefano GDS 1201 CD: Rodolphe RPC 32484-32487 CD: Melodram CDM 26013 CD: Laserlight 15096 CD: Hallmark 390362/311102 Fragment of Casta diva from this performance also exists on newsreel film
Milan December 1955	Carturan, Simionato, Del Monaco, Zaccaria La Scala Orchestra & Chorus Votto	LP: BJR Records BJR 147 LP: Limited Edition Society 103 CD: Hunt CD 517/CDHP 517 CD: Legendary LRCD 1007 Excerpts LP: Dei della musica 2 LP: Paragon DSV 52014

Rome
January
1958
	Pirazzini,
	Corelli, Neri
	Rome Opera
	Orchestra & Chorus
	Santini
		LP: Morgan MOR 5801
		LP: Voce 8
		LP: Great Operatic Performances
		    GFC 008-009
		CD: Melodram MEL 16000
		Act 1 only performed on this occasion
		Excerpts
		LP: Historical Recording Enterprises
		    HRE 263
		LP: Dei della musica 10

Norma/concluded

Milan
September
1960
	Vincenzi,
	C.Ludwig, Corelli,
	Zaccaria
	La Scala
	Orchestra & Chorus
	Serafin
		LP: Columbia 33CX 1766-1768/
		    SAX 2412-2414
		LP: Columbia (Germany) C 91192-91194/
		    STC 91192-91194
		LP: Columbia (France) CCA 891-893
		LP: Angel 3615
		LP: EMI 2C 165 00535-00537/
		    3C 163 00535-00537/SLS 5186
		CD: EMI CMS 763 0002
		<u>Excerpts</u>
		LP: Columbia (Germany) C 80689/
		    C 80729/SMC 80729
		LP: Columbia (France) CC 130550
		LP: Angel 35666/36818/3743
		LP: EMI ASD 3908/SHZE 101/1C063 00730/
		    2C 069 01342/2C 059 43263/143 2631
		CD: EMI CDC 749 5022/CDC 754 7022/
		    CDC 252 9382/CMS 565 7462/
		    CMS 565 9522
		CD: Palladio PD 4170

Paris May 1965	Bellary, Simionato/Cossotto, Cecchele, Vinco Paris Opéra Orchestra & Chorus Prêtre	CD: Eklipse EKR 18 CD: Gala GL 100.523 <u>Existing recording, drawn from performances</u> <u>between 14-29 May, are incomplete (these</u> <u>two issues vary in content)</u> <u>Excerpts</u> LP: Opus 92/IGS 001/TCC 500 LP: Historical Recording Enterprises HRE 219/HRE 263/HRE 373 CD: Melodram CDM 16038 CD: Legendary LRCD 1009

Norma, excerpt (Oh rimembranza!)

Buenos Aires June 1949	Barbieri Teatro Colon Orchestra Serafin	LP: Historical Recording Enterprises HRE 373 CD: Melodram MEL 36513 CD: Eklipse EKR 33 CD: Gala GL 316

Norma, excerpt (Casta diva)

Turin November 1949	RAI Torino Orchestra Basile	78: Cetra 20482 78: Parlophone R 30041 LP: Cetra LPC 55057 LP: FWR 646/OASI 532 LP: Morgan A 006 LP: Foyer FO 1007 CD: Foyer 2CF-2020 CD: Cetra CDC 5 CD: Melodram MEL 26034 CD: Verona 27058-27059 CD: Great Opera Performances GOP 741 CD: Fabbri GVS 03
London September 1958	Orchestra Pritchard	LP: Voce 18 CD: Legato LCD 162 Televised performance

Paris
December
1958
	Mars
	Paris Opéra
	Orchestra & Chorus
	Sébastian
		LP: Historical Operatic Treasures
		    ERR 118
		LP: Historical Recording Enterprises
		    HRE 242
		LP: Foyer FO 1006
		CD: Foyer CDS 16010
		CD: Rodolphe RPC 32495
		CD: Gala GL 324
		CD: Memories HR 4293-4294
		CD: Great Opera Performances GOP 748
		VHS Video: EMI MVD 991 2583
		Laserdisc: EMI LDB 991 2581
		Also issued on CD by Frequenz

Berlin May 1963	Deutsche Oper Orchestra Prêtre	CD: Eklipse EKR 33
Stuttgart May 1963	SDR Orchestra Prêtre	LP: Voce 34 CD: Melodram MEL 26035 CD: Eklipse EKR 13
London May 1963	Philharmonia Prêtre	Unpublished private recording
Paris May 1964	Paris Opéra Orchestra & Chorus Prêtre	Unpublished video recording Incomplete newsreel film (recitative only)

Paris versions of the aria include opening recitative Sediziosi voci;
unspecified versions of Casta diva on CDs Javelin HADCD 116 and Newsound
PNCD 0101

Postage stamps with Maria Callas from Greece and Nicaragua

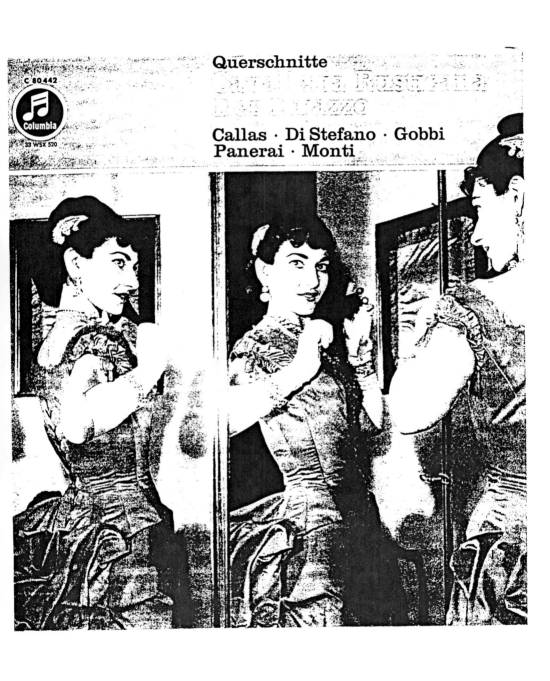

Querschnitte

C 80442

Columbia

33 WSX 520

Callas · Di Stefano · Gobbi
Panerai · Monti

Il pirata

New York January 1959	Role of Imogene Ferraro, Ego American Opera Society Orchestra and Chorus Rescigno	LP: FWR 641 LP: MRF Records MRF 51 LP: BJR Records BJR 145 LP: Replica RPL 2487-2489 CD: Hunt CD 531/CDHP 531 CD: Melodram MEL 26013 CD: EMI CMS 764 9382 Excerpts LP: BJR Records BJR 143 LP: Historical Recording Enterprises HRE 219 LP: Dei della musica 11 LP: Gioielli della lirica GML 34 LP: Foyer FO 1007 CD: Foyer 2CF-2020

Il pirata, excerpt (Sorgete, è in me dover)

London
November
1961
	Sinclair, Young
	Philharmonia
	Tonini
		LP: EMI ASD 2791/1C 063 03253/
		    2C 069 03253/3C 065 03253/
		    2C 165 54178-54188
		LP: Angel 36852
		CD: EMI CDC 747 2832/CDS 749 4532

Il pirata, excerpt (Col sorriso d'innocenza)

London
September
1958
	Philharmonia
	Rescigno
		LP: Columbia 33CX 1654/SAX 2320
		LP: Angel 36930
		LP: EMI 1C 063 00784/2C 069 00784/
		    3C 065 00784/2C165 54178-54188
		CD: EMI CDC 747 2832/CDS 749 4532/
		    CMS 763 2442

Hamburg May 1959	NDR Orchestra Rescigno	LP: Historical Recording Enterprises HRE 228 LP: Rodolphe RP 12382 CD: Arkadia 4101 CD: Frequenz CMH 1 CD: Virtuoso 269.7122 CD: Great Opera Performances GOP 748 CD: Gala GL 325 Laserdisc: Pioneer (Japan) PA 85-150 VHS Video: EMI MVD 491 7113
Stuttgart May 1959	SDR Orchestra Rescigno	LP: Voce 18 CD: Eklipse EKR 37
Amsterdam July 1959	Concertgebouw Orchestra Rescigno	LP: BJR Records BJR 103 LP: Voce 34 LP: Melodram MEL 079 LP: Collectors Limited Edition RPCL 2056 CD: Cetra CDC 4 CD: Rodolphe RPC 32484-32487 CD: EMI CDC 749 4282
London September 1959	LSO Rescigno	LP: Opera Dubs OD 101-2 Opening recitative only from an amateur recording

I puritani

Mexico City May 1952	Role of Elvira Di Stefano, Campolonghi, Silva, Ruffino Bellas Artes Orchestra & Chorus Picco	LP: Ed Smith UORC 191 LP: MRF Records MRF 28 LP: Cetra LO 52 CD: Melodram MEL 26027 Excerpts LP: Legendary Recordings LR 151 CD: Melodram MEL 26023/MEL 36513 CD: Memories HR 4372-4373 CD: Verona 28007-28009

Milan
March 1953
	Di Stefano,
	Panerai, Forti,
	Rossi-Lemeni
	La Scala
	Orchestra & Chorus
	Serafin
		LP: Columbia 33CX 1058-1060
		LP: Columbia (Germany) C 90315-90317
		LP: Angel 3502
		LP: EMI 2C 163 00406-00408/
		    2C 163 52780-52787/
		    3C 163 00406-00408/SLS 5140/
		    EX 29 08743
		CD: EMI CDS 747 3088/CDS 556 2752/
		    CMS 252 9432
		Excerpts
		45: Columbia SEL 1550/SEL 1554
		LP: Columbia (Germany) C 80448/C 80602
		LP: Angel 35304/36940/3743
		LP: EMI 1C 191 01433-01434M/
		    1C 191 01593-01594M/3C 063 01510/
		    3C 065 01016/3C 065 17902/SLS 856/
		    SLS 5057/SLS 5104
		CD: EMI CDM 769 5432/CDS 754 1032/
		    CMS 763 2442/CMS 565 5342/
		    CZS 252 1642

I puritani, excerpt (Oh vieni al tempio!)

Milan September 1956	RAI Milano Orchestra Simonetto	LP: BJR Records BJR 143 LP: Morgan A 006 LP: Timaclub 16 LP: Melodram MEL 079 LP: Legendary Recordings LR 151 LP: Foyer FO 1007 CD: Foyer 2CF-2020 CD: Rodolphe RPC 32484-32487 CD: Cetra CDC 4/CDMR 5007 CD: Memories HR 4293-4294 CD: Verona 27058-27059 CD: Hunt CD 537/CDHP 537 CD: Great Opera Performances GOP 730 CD: Gala GL 100.515

I puritani, excerpt (Qui la voce)

Turin November 1949	RAI Torino Orchestra Basile	78: Cetra 20483 78: Parlophone R 30043 LP: Cetra LPC 50175/LPC 55041/LPC 55057 LP: OASI 532 LP: Everest SDBR 3259/SDBR 3293 LP: Ember GVC 16 LP: Turnabout THS 65125 CD: Rodolphe RPC 32484-32487 CD: Cetra CDC 5/CDO 104 CD: Foyer CDS 15001 CD: Nimbus NI 7864 CD: Verona 27058-27059 CD: Palladio PD 4137 CD: Andromeda ANR 2518-2519 CD: Priceless D 18363 CD: Memories HR 4293-4294 CD: Fabbri GVS 03
Dallas November 1957	Dallas Civic Opera Orchestra Rescigno	LP: FWR 646/FWR 656 LP: BJR Records BJR 143 LP: Historical Recording Enterprises HRE 219/HRE 232 LP: Collectors Limited Edition MDTP 028 LP: Melodram MEL 26016 LP: Legato LCD 131 LP: Paragon DSV 52014 CD: Verona 28007-28009 CD: Gala GL 323 CD: Great Opera Performances GOP 724 Rehearsal performance (BJR edition is spliced together as a continuous performance)

La sonnambula

Milan
March 1955
	<u>Role of Amina</u>
	Ratti, Valletti,
	Modesti
	La Scala
	Orchestra & Chorus
	Bernstein
		LP: Historical Operatic Treasures
		    ERR 108
		LP: BJR Records BJR 138
		LP: Raritas OPR 3
		CD: Documents LV 955-956
		CD: Myto MCD 89006
		<u>Excerpts</u>
		LP: Limited Edition Records 100
		LP: Historical Recording Enterprises
		    HRE 219
		CD: Hunt CD 517
		CD: Fabbri GVS 03
		<u>CD 517 incorrectly dated 1957</u>

Milan
March 1957
	Cossotto, Monti,
	Zaccaria
	La Scala
	Orchestra & Chorus
	Votto
		LP: Columbia 33CX 1469-1471
		LP: Columbia (Germany) C 90555-90557
		LP: Angel 3568/6108
		LP: EMI 2C 163 17648-17650/
		    2C163 18359-18360/2C163 52780-52787/
		    3C163 17648-17650/EX 29 00433
		CD: EMI CDS 747 3788/CDS 556 2782/
		    CMS 252 9432
		<u>Excerpts</u>
		LP: Columbia 33CX 1540
		LP: Columbia (Germany) C 80448/C 80602
		LP: Angel 35304/36929
		LP: EMI 3C 063 00741/3C 063 01016/
		    3C 063 17920
		CD: EMI CDC 749 5022/CMS 763 2442/
		    CMS 565 5342/CZS 252 1642

Cologne July 1957 (4 July)	Cossotto, Monti, Zaccaria La Scala Orchestra & Chorus Votto	LP: BJR Records BJR 152 CD: Hunt CD 503 CD: Melodram MEL 26003 CD: Hunt CDHP 503 CD: Verona 2704-2705 <u>Excerpts</u> LP: Legendary Recordings LR 151 LP: Gioielli della lirica GML 09 LP: Paragon DSV 52014 CD: Cetra CDC 4 CD: Foyer CDS 15002 CD: Myto MCD 89006 CD: Hallmark 390362/311092/311112

La sonnambula/concluded

Cologne July 1957 (6 July)	Cossotto, Monti, Zaccaria La Scala Orchestra & Chorus Votto	LP: Foyer FO 1005 Excerpts CD: Eklipse EKR 12
Edinburgh August 1957	Cossotto, Monti, Zaccaria La Scala Orchestra & Chorus Votto	LP: Limited Edition Society 104 CD: Virtuoso 269.7252 Excerpts LP: Dei della musica 15 CD: Rodolphe RPC 32484-32487 CD: Eklipse EKR 12 EKR 12 states that the excerpts are from a second Edinburgh performance

La sonnambula, excerpt (Come per me sereno)

Milan
June 1955
	La Scala
	Orchestra
	Serafin
		LP: Penzance PR 15
		LP: Morgan MOR 5401
		LP: FWR 644
		LP: EMI ASD 3535/1C 063 01299/
		    2C 069 01299/3C 065 01299/
		    2C 165 54178-54188
		LP: Angel 37557
		CD: EMI CDC 747 9662/CDS 749 4532/
		    CDC 555 0162/CDM 565 7472/
		    CMS 565 7462

La sonnambula, excerpt (Ah non credea mirarti/Ah non giunge!)

Milan
June 1955
	La Scala
	Orchestra
	Serafin
		LP: Penzance PR 15
		LP: Morgan MOR 5401
		LP: FWR 656
		LP: EMI ASD 3535/1C 069 01299/
		    2C 069 01299/3C 065 01299/
		    2C 165 54178-54188
		LP: Angel 37557
		CD: EMI CDC 747 9662/CDS 749 4532/
		    CDS 555 0162/CDM 565 7472/
		    CMS 565 7462/CMS 565 9522

Paris May 1965	Orchestre National Prêtre	LP: Historical Recording Enterprises HRE 263 CD: Melodram MEL 36513 VHS Video: Bel Canto Society BCS 0199 Televised performance without cabaletta

HECTOR BERLIOZ (1803–1869)

La damnation de Faust, excerpt (D'amour l'ardente flamme)

Paris
May 1963
	Conservatoire
	Orchestra
	Prêtre
		LP: Columbia 33CX 1858/SAX 2503
		LP: Columbia (Germany) C 91246/STC 91246
		LP: Columbia (France) CVB 975
		LP: Angel 36147/3696/3950
		LP: EMI 1C 065 00578/2C 069 00578/
		    2C 165 54178-54188/3C 065 00578/
		    1C 187 01398-01399
		CD: EMI CDC 749 0592/CDS 749 4532/
		    CDS 754 1032

GEORGES BIZET (1838–1875)

Paris
July 1964
	Role of Carmen
	Guiot, Gedda,
	Massard
	Paris Opéra
	Orchestra & Chorus
	Prêtre
		LP: EMI AN 143-145/SAN 143-145/
		    CAN 140-142/SMA 91392-91394/
		    1C 165 00034-00036/
		    2C167 00034-00036/3C163 00034-00036/
		    SLS 913/EX 29 08803
		LP: Angel 3650
		CD: EMI CDS 747 3138/CDS 754 3682/
		    CDS 556 2812/CMS 252 9432
		Excerpts
		LP: EMI ALP 2282/ASD 2282/SMC 80866/
		    CVT 3552/1C 063 01966/
		    1C 187 01398-01399/2C 069 43088/
		    3C 065 00304/2C 059 43263/
		    143 2631
		LP: Angel 36312/36361/3800/6062
		CD: EMI CDC 749 5022/CDC 555 0162/
		    CDC 555 2162/CMS 565 5342/
		    CMS 565 7462/CMS 565 9522/
		    CZS 252 6142

Carmen, excerpt (C'est toi! C'est moi!)

Tokyo October 1974	Di Stefano Sutherland, piano	CD: Cin CCCD 1037-1038 Also unpublished video recording
Montreal May 1974	Di Stefano Sutherland, piano	CD: Fonovox 78122

Carmen, excerpt (L'amour est un oiseau rebelle)

Paris
March–
April 1961
	Orchestre
	National
	Prêtre
		LP: Columbia 33CX 1771/SAX 2410
		LP: Columbia (Germany) C 91155/STC 91155
		LP: Columbia (France) CVB 902
		LP: Angel 35882/36135/3696
		LP: EMI 2C 069 00540/3C 065 00540/
		    2C 165 54178-54188/SHZE 101/
		    SXLP 30166/EMX 2123 /ASD 4306
		CD: EMI CDC 749 0592/CDC 252 9382/
		    CDC 754 7022/CMS 565 7462/
		    CDEMX 2123/CMS 565 9522/CDS 749 4532
		
		SAX 2410 also re-issued by Testament
		in an audiophile LP edition

Hamburg March 1962	NDR Orchestra Prêtre	LP: MRF Records MRF 83 LP: Voce 34 CD: Arkadia 4101 CD: Frequenz CMH 1 CD: Foyer CDS 15003 CD: Virtuoso 269.7122 CD: Great Opera Performances GOP 748 CD: Gala GL 322 Laserdisc: Pioneer (Japan) PA 85-150 VHS Video: EMI MVD 491 7113
New York May 1962	Wilson, piano	LP: Legendary Recordings LR 111 CD: Ornamenti 109
London November 1962	Covent Garden Orchestra Prêtre	LP: Historical Recording Enterprises HRE 219 CD: Verona 27058-27059 Laserdisc: EMI LDB 491 2831 VHS Video: EMI MVD 491 2833
Brookville NY April 1974	Sutherland, piano	CD: Legato LCD 137
Tokyo October 1974	Sutherland, piano	LP: Historical Recording Enterprises HRE 323 CD: Cin CCCD 1037-1038 Also unpublished video recording
Montreal May 1974	Di Stefano Sutherland, piano	CD: Fonovox 78122

Carmen, excerpt (Près des remparts de Séville)

Paris
March–
April 1961
	Orchestre
	National
	Prêtre
		LP: Columbia 33CX 1771/SAX 2410
		LP: Columbia (Germany) C 91155/STC 91155
		LP: Columbia (France) CVB 902
		LP: Angel 35882/3696
		LP: EMI 2C 069 00540/3C 065 00540/
		    2C 165 54178-54188/SHZE 101/
		    SXLP 30166/EMX 2123/ASD 4306
		CD: EMI CDC 749 0592/CDC 252 9382/
		    CDS 749 4532/CDEMX 2123
		SAX 2410 also re-issued by Testament
		as an audiophile LP edition

Hamburg March 1962	NDR Orchestra Prêtre	LP: MRF Records MRF 83 LP: Voce 34 CD: Arkadia 4101 CD: Frequenz CMH 1 CD: Foyer CDS 15003 CD: Virtuoso 269.7122 CD: Great Opera Performances GOP 74ρ CD: Gala GL 322 Laserdisc: Pioneer (Japan) PA 85-150 VHS Video: EMI MVD 491 7113
New York May 1962	Wilson, piano	LP: Legendary Recordings LR 111 CD: Ornamenti 109
London November 1962	Covent Garden Orchestra Prêtre	LP: Historical Recording Enterprises CD: Verona 27058-27059 Laserdisc: EMI LDB 491 2831 VHS Video: EMI MVD 491 2833

Les pêcheurs de perles, excerpt (Comme autrefois)

Paris
May 1963
	Conservatoire
	Orchestra
	Prêtre
		LP: Columbia 33CX 1859/SAX 2503
		LP: Columbia (Germany) C 91246/STC 91246
		LP: Columbia (France) CVB 975
		LP: Angel 36147/3950
		LP: EMI 1C 065 00578/2C 069 00578/
		    3C 065 00578/2C 165 54178-54188/
		    1C 187 01398-01399
		CD: EMI CDC 749 0592/CDS 749 4532

ARRIGO BOITO (1842–1918)

Mefistofele, excerpt (L'altra notte)

Watford September 1954	Philharmonia Serafin	45: Columbia SEL 1581 LP: Columbia 33CX 1231 LP: Columbia (Germany) C 90409 LP: Columbia (France) FCX 30088 LP: Angel 35233 LP: EMI 1C 053 01013M/3C 065 01013/ 2C 165 54178–54188/SLS 869/ASD 3824 CD: EMI CDC 747 2882/CDS 749 4532
London October 1959	RPO Sargent	LP: BJR Records BJR 143 LP: Legendary Recordings LR 148 LP: Foyer FO 1007 CD: Foyer 2CF-2020 CD: Legato LCD 162 CD: Melodram MEL 26034 CD: Great Opera Performances GOP 741 CD: Gala GL 316 <u>Televised performance</u>
London May 1961	Sargent, piano	LP: Penzance PR 15 LP: Historical Recording Enterprises HRE 219 CD: Legato LCD 162

ALFREDO CATALANI (1854–1893)

La Wally, excerpt (Ebben? Ne andrò lontana)

Watford
September
1954
	Philharmonia
	Serafin
		LP: Columbia 33CX 1231
		LP: Columbia (Germany) C 90409
		LP: Columbia (France) FCX 30088
		LP: Angel 35233
		LP: EMI 1C 053 01013M/3C 065 01013/
		    2C 165 54178–54188/SLS 869/ASD 3824
		CD: EMI CDC 747 2822 /CDC 754 4022/
		    CDC 749 5022/CDS 749 4532/
		    CMS 565 7462/CMS 565 9522
		CD Single: EMI 881 2992

MARIA CALLAS AT COVENT GARDEN

Maria Callas made her debut at Covent Garden on 8 November 1952,
singing the title role in *Norma*, and her final appearance was on
5 July 1965, in the title role of *Tosca*.

Performances she gave at the Royal Opera House were:

Norma
8, 10, 13, 18, 20 November 1952
15, 17, 20, 23 June 1953
Norma Maria Callas
Adalgisa Ebe Stignani/Giulietta Simionato
Pollione Mirto Picchi
Oroveso Giacomo Vaghi/Giulio Neri
Conductor Vittorio Gui/John Pritchard

Il trovatore
26, 29 June, 1 July 1953
Leonora Maria Callas
Azucena Giulietta Simionato
Manrico James Johnston
Count di Luna Jess Walters
Conductor Alberto Erede

Aida
4, 6, 10 June 1953
Aida Maria Callas
Amneris Giulietta Simionato
Radames Kurt Baum
Amonasro Jess Walters
Conductor John Barbirolli

Norma
2, 6 February 1957
Norma Maria Callas
Adalgisa Ebe Stignani
Pollione Giuseppe Vertecchi
Oroveso Nicola Zaccaria
Conductor John Pritchard

I Puritani
10 June 1958 (Gala Performance in
calebration of the Centenary of the
Royal Opera House)
Elvira Maria Callas
Conductor John Pritchard

La traviata
20, 23, 26, 28, 30 June 1958
Violetta Maria Callas
Alfredo Cesare Valletti
Giorgio Germont Mario Zanasi
Conductor Nicola Rescigno

Medea
17, 22, 24, 27, 30 June 1959
Medea Maria Callas
Neris Fiorenza Cossotto
Jason Jon Vickers
Creon Nicola Zaccaria
Conductor Nicola Rescigno

Tosca
21, 24, 27, 30 January 1, 5 February 1964
Tosca Maria Callas
Cavaradossi Renato Cioni
Scarpia Tito Gobbi
Conductor Carlo Felice Cillario

Tosca
5 July 1965 (Royal Opera House
Benevolent Fund Gala)
Tosca Maria Callas
Cavaradossi Renato Cioni
Scarpia Tito Gobbi
Conductor Georges Prêtre

Royal Opera House

COVENT GARDEN

HOUSE MANAGER . JOHN COLLINS

THE ROYAL OPERA HOUSE, COVENT GARDEN LIMITED

GENERAL ADMINISTRATOR . DAVID L. WEBSTER

in association with the Arts Council of Great Britain

presents

THE COVENT GARDEN OPERA

in

the first performance of a new production of

MEDEA

Opera in Three Acts

Music *by* LUIGI CHERUBINI
(Property of G. Ricordi & Co.)

Text *by* FRANÇOIS BENOIT HOFFMANN

Recitatives by FRANZ LACHNER

Italian translation by CARLO ZANGARINI

Lighting by WILLIAM BUNDY

Conductor — **NICOLA RESCIGNO**

Producer — **ALEXIS MINOTIS**
of the Royal Theatre of Greece

Scenery and Costumes by **JOHN TSAROUCHIS**

on

WEDNESDAY, 17th JUNE, 1959

GUSTAVE CHARPENTIER (1860–1950)

Louise, excerpt (Depuis le jour)

San Remo December 1954	RAI Milano Orchestra Simonetto	LP: Historical Operatic Treasures ERR 134 LP: BJR Records BJR 143 LP: Timaclub 16 LP: Foyer FO 1007 CD: Foyer 2CF-2020/CDS 15006 CD: Cetra CDC 5/CDMR 5002 CD: Laserlight 15224 CD: Memories HR 4419-4420 CD: Rodolphe RPC 32484-32487 CD: Verona 27058-27059 CD: Gala GL 100.515 CD: Great Opera Performances GOP 730 CD: Hunt CD 536/CDHP 536 CD: Newsound PNCD 0101 CD: Hallmark 390362/311092

Paris
March–
April 1961
	Orchestre
	National
	Prêtre
		LP: Columbia 33CX 1771/SAX 2410
		LP: Columbia (Germany) C 91155/STC 91155
		LP: Columbia (France) CVB 902
		LP: Angel 35882/3696/3950
		LP: EMI 2C 069 00540/3C 065 00540/
		    2C 165 54178-54188/SXLP 30166/
		    EMX 2123/ASD 4306
		CD: EMI CDC 749 0592/CDC 555 0162/
		    CDS 749 4532/CDS 754 1032/
		    CMS 565 7462/CDEMX 2123
		SAX 2410 also re-issued by Testament
		as an audiophile LP edition

LUIGI CHERUBINI (1760-1842)

Medea

Florence May 1953	Role of Medea Tucci, Barbieri, Guichandut, Petri Maggio musicale Orchestra & Chorus Gui	CD: Hunt CD 516/CDHP 516
Milan December 1953	Nache, Barbieri, Penno, Modesti La Scala Orchestra & Chorus Bernstein	LP: Ed Smith UORC 128 LP: BJR Records BJR 129 LP: MRF Records MRF 102 LP: Morgan MOR 5301 LP: Melodram MEL 404 CD: Cetra CDE 1019 CD: Melodram MEL 26022 CD: Verona 27088-27089 Excerpts LP: Historical Recording Enterprises HRE 219 LP: Dei della musica 12 CD: Laserlight 15096 CD: Fabbri GVS 03 CD: Hallmark 390362/311092
Milan September 1957	Scotto, Pirazzini, Picchi, Modesti La Scala Orchestra & Chorus Serafin	LP: Columbia 33CX 1618-1620/ SAX 2290-2292 LP: Ricordi OS 101-103/AOCL 316001 LP: Mercury SR 39000/OL3-104 LP: Everest 327/S-437 LP: Cetra DOCL 201 CD: EMI CMS 763 6252 Excerpts LP: Mercury MG 50233/SR 90233 LP: Everest SDBR 7437/SDBR 3293/SDBR 3364 LP: Elite Special RLP 2 LP: Rodolphe RP 12376 CD: EMI CMS 763 2442

Dallas
November
1958
	Carron, Berganza,
	Vickers, Zaccaria
	Dallas Civic
	Opera Orchestra
	and Chorus
	Rescigno
		LP: FWR 647
		LP: Penzance PR 41
		LP: Robin Hood RHR 512
		LP: Collectors Limited Editions
		    AMDRL 32817
		LP: Historical Recording Enterprises
		    HRE 358
		CD: Melodram MEL 26016
		CD: Gala GL 100.521

Medea/concluded

London June 1959	Carlyle, Cossotto, Vickers, Zaccaria Covent Garden Orchestra & Chorus Rescigno	LP: BJR Records BJR 105 LP: Foyer FO 1001 CD: Melodram MEL 26005 CD: Curcio-Hunt OPI 10 CD: Hunt CDMP 464 CD: Virtuoso 269.7262 Excerpts LP: Gioielli della lirica GML 49 CD: Foyer CDS 15003/CDS 15006 CD: Hallmark 390362/311102/ 311112
Milan December 1961	Tosini, Simionato, Vickers, Ghiaurov La Scala Orchestra & Chorus Schippers	LP: MRF Records MRF 102 CD: Hunt CDLSMH 34028/CDMP 428 Excerpts CD: Memories HR 4394-4395

Medea, excerpt (Dei tuoi figli)

Milan
June 1955
	La Scala
	Orchestra
	Serafin
		LP: Columbia 33CX 1540
		LP: Columbia (Germany) C 80448
		LP: Angel 35304
		LP: EMI 1C 053 01016M/3C 065 01016/
		    2C 165 54178-54188
		CD: EMI CDC 747 2822/CDS 749 4532/
		    CDS 749 6002/CDS 754 1032/
		    CMS 565 5342/CZS 252 1642
		CD: Rodolphe RPC 32484-32487

FRANCESCO CILEA (1866–1950)

Adriana Lecouvreur, excerpt (Io son l'umile ancella)

Watford	Philharmonia	45: Columbia SEL 1581
September	Serafin	LP: Columbia 33CX 1231
1954		LP: Columbia (Germany) C 90409
		LP: Columbia (France) FCX 30088
		LP: Angel 35233
		LP: EMI 1C 053 01013M/3C 065 01013/
		2C 165 54178-54188/SLS 869/ASD 3824
		CD: EMI CDC 747 2822/CDC 555 0162/
		CDS 749 4532/CMS 565 7462

Adriana Lecouvreur, excerpt (Poveri fiori)

Watford	Philharmonia	45: Columbia SEL 1581
September	Serafin	LP: Columbia 33CX 1231
1954		LP: Columbia (Germany) C 90409
		LP: Columbia (France) FCX 30088
		LP: Angel 35233
		LP: EMI 1C 053 01013M/3C 065 01013/
		2C 165 54178-54188/SLS 869/ASD 3824
		CD: EMI CDC 747 2822/CDS 749 4532

LEO DELIBES (1836–1891)

Lakmé, excerpt (Où va la jeune Indoue?)

Turin February 1952	RAI Torino Orchestra De Fabritiis Sung in Italian	LP: Limited Edition Records 100 LP: BJR Records BJR 143 LP: Timaclub 16 LP: Historical Recording Enterprises HRE 219 LP: Foyer FO 1007 CD: Foyer 2CF-2020 CD: Cetra CDC 5/CDMR 5001 CD: Rodolphe RPC 32484-32487 CD: Verona 27058-27059 CD: Hunt CD 536/CDHP 536 CD: Great Opera Performances GOP 730 CD: Gala GL 100.515

Watford
September
1954
	Philharmonia
	Serafin
	Sung in Italian
		LP: Columbia 33CX 1231
		LP: Columbia (Germany) C 90409
		LP: Columbia (France) FCX 30088
		LP: Angel 35233
		LP: EMI 1C 053 01013M/3C 065 01013/
		    2C 165 54178-54188/ASD 3824/
		    SLS 5018/SLS 5057
		CD: EMI CDC 747 2822/CDC 555 2162/
		    CDM 565 7472/CDS 749 4532/
		    CMS 565 5342/CMS 565 7462/
		    CZS 252 6142

GAETONO DONIZETTI (1797-1848)

Anna Bolena

Milan April 1957	<u>Role of Anna</u> Simionato, G.Raimondi, Rossi-Lemeni, Clabassi La Scala Orchestra & Chorus Gavazzeni	LP: FWR 646 LP: BJR Records BJR 109 LP: MRF Records MRF 42 LP: Morgan MOR 5703 LP: Foyer FO 1014 CD: Hunt CD 518/CDHP 518 CD: Melodram MEL 26010 CD: EMI CMS 764 9412 CD: Great Opera Performances GOP 768 CD: Verona 27090-27091 <u>Excerpts</u> LP: Historical Recording Enterprises HRE 219 LP: Musidisc SC 8221 LP: Dei della musica 6 LP: Foyer FO 1007 LP: Paragon DSV 52014 CD: Fabbri GVS 03 CD: Hallmark 390362/311112 CD: Foyer 2CF-2020/CDS 15002 CD: Memories HR 4574-4575

Anna Bolena, excerpt (Al dolce guidami)

Dallas November 1957	Dallas Civic Opera Orchestra & Chorus Rescigno	LP: FWR 646/MDTP 028 LP: Historical Recording Enterprises HRE 232 CD: Verona 28007-28009 CD: Legato LCD 131 CD: Great Opera Performances GOP 724 CD: Gala GL 323 <u>Rehearsal performance</u>
London June 1958	Sinclair, Lanigan, Rouleau, Robertson Philharmonia Orchestra & Chorus Rescigno	LP: Columbia 33CX 1654/SAX 2320 LP: Columbia (Germany) C 70413 LP: Angel 36930 LP: EMI 1C 063 00784/2C 069 00784/ 3C065 00784/2C165 54178-54188 CD: EMI CDC 747 2832/CDS 749 4532/ CMS 763 2442
London February 1962	Philharmonia Prêtre	LP: Opera Dubs OD 101-2 LP: Melodram MEL 674 CD: Melodram MEL 36513

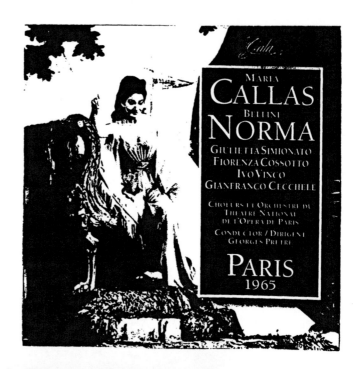

DONIZETTI
LUCIA DI LAMMERMOOR

MARIA MENEGHINI CALLAS
GIUSEPPE DI STEFANO
TITO GOBBI

ORCHESTRA AND CHORUS OF THE
FLORENCE 'MAGGIO MUSICALE'
conductor
TULLIO SERAFIN

COLUMBIA
LONG PLAYING 33⅓ R.P.M. RECORD

L'elisir d'amore, excerpt (Prendi per me)

Paris	Conservatoire	LP: Columbia 33CX 1923/SAX 2564
December	Orchestra	LP: Columbia (Germany) STC 91410
1963-	Rescigno	LP: Angel 36239
April 1964		LP: EMI 2C 069 00592/3C 065 00592/
		2C 165 54178-54188
		CD: EMI CDC 747 2832/CDS 749 4532/
		CDM 565 7472

L'elisir d'amore, excerpt (Una parola, Adina!)

London	Di Stefano	Philips unpublished
November-	LSO	Recording incomplete
December	Almeida	
1972		
Hamburg	Di Stefano	LP: TCC 501
October	Newton, piano	CD: Eklipse EKR 33
1973		
Brookville NY	Di Stefano	CD: Legato LCD 137
April 1974	Sutherland, piano	
Cincinnati	Di Stefano	CD: Verona 28007-28009
April 1974	Sutherland, piano	
Tokyo	Di Stefano	LP: Historical Recording Enterprises
October	Sutherland, piano	HRE 323
1974		CD: Cin CCCD 1037-1038
		Also unpublished video recording

La figlia del reggimento, excerpt (Convien partir)

Paris	Conservatoire	LP: Columbia 33CX 1923/SAX 2564
December	Orchestra	LP: Columbia (Germany) STC 91410
1963-	Rescigno	LP: Angel 36239/3743
April 1964		LP: EMI 2C 069 00592/3C 065 00592/
		2C 165 54178-54188
		CD: EMI CDC 747 2832/CDS 749 4532

Lucia di Lammermoor

Mexico City June 1952 (10 June)	<u>Role of Lucia</u> Di Stefano, Del Monte, Silva, Campolonghi Bellas Artes Orchestra & Chorus Picco	LP: FWR 650 LP: Historical Recording Enterprises HRE 256 CD: Myto MCD 91340 Excerpts LP: Rodolphe RP 22413-22415 CD: Rodolphe RPC 22413-22415 CD: Melodram MEL 26021 CD: Verona 28007-28009 CD: Memories HR 4581 HR 4581 contains Mad scene and encored version from the same performance

Florence
February
1953
	Di Stefano, Gobbi,
	Arié, Natali
	Maggio musicale
	Orchestra & Chorus
	Serafin
		LP: Columbia 33CX 1131-1132
		LP: Angel 3503/6032
		LP: EMI 1C 137 00942-00943M/
		    2C163 00942-00943/3C165 00942-00943
		CD: EMI CMS 769 9802
		Excerpts
		45: Columbia SEL 1522
		LP: Columbia 33CX 1385
		LP: EMI 1C 153 52287-52288/
		    3C 065 17902
		CD: EMI CMS 763 2442/CMS 565 5342/
		    CZS 252 6142/CMS 764 4182

Milan January 1954	Di Stefano, Zampieri, Panerai, Modesti La Scala Orchestra & Chorus Karajan	CD: Legato SRO 831 Excerpts LP: Cetra ARK 5 LP: Fonola ST 5010 LP: Historical Recording Enterprises HRE 219 LP: Dei della musica 13

Lucia di Lammermoor/continued

Berlin September 1955	Di Stefano, Villa, Zaccaria, Panerai La Scala Chorus RIAS Orchestra Karajan	LP: Limited Edition Society LER 101 LP: BJR Records BJR 143 LP: Morgan MOR 5401 LP: Cetra LO 18/ARK 5 LP: Turnabout THS 65144-65145 LP: Replica ARPL 32495 LP: Paragon DSV 52004 LP: Rodolphe RPV 32667-32668 LP: Movimento musica 02.001 CD: Melodram MEL 26004 CD: Hunt CD 502/CDHP 502 CD: Movimento musica 012.010 CD: Verona 2709-2710 CD: Virtuoso 269.7232 CD: Palette PAL 2009-2010 CD: Rodolphe RPL 32518/RPV 32667-32668 CD: EMI CMS 763 6312 Excerpts LP: Limited Edition Society LER 100 LP: Rodolphe RP 12701 LP: Ricordi OCL 16331 LP: Joker SM 1298 LP: Gioielli della lirica GML 1 LP: Melodiya M10 44825 LP: Paragon DSV 52014 CD: Fabbri GSV 03 CD: Movimento musica 011.002 CD: Rodolphe RPC 32484-32487 CD: Foyer CDS 15002/CDS 15004 CD: Natise HVK 110 CD: Virtuoso 269.7112 CD: Cetra CDE 1027/CDS 51027 CD: Memories HR 4293-4294/HR 4372-4373
Naples March 1956 (22 March)	G.Raimondi, Borrelli, Panerai, Zerbini San Carlo Orchestra & Chorus Molinari-Pradelli	LP: Opera Dubs OD 100 CD: Myto MCD 90319 Excerpts CD: Melodram MEL 36513
New York December 1956	Campora, Sordello, Moscona Metropolitan Opera Orchestra & Chorus Cleva	LP: Raritas OPR 412 LP: Melodram MEL 010 CD: Melodram MEL 26034

Lucia di Lammermoor/concluded

Rome June 1957	Fernandi, Panerai, Modesti,Formichini RAI Roma Orchestra & Chorus Serafin	LP: Historical Recording Enterprises HRE 221 LP: Replica RPL 2419-2421 CD: Melodram 26014 CD: Hunt CDLSMH 34022 Excerpts LP: BJR Records BJR 133 LP: Dei della musica 3 CD: Laserlight 15096 CD: Memories HR 4444-4445 CD: Hallmark 390362/311112

London
March 1959
	Tagliavini,
	Cappuccilli,
	Ladysz
	Philharmonia
	Orchestra & Chorus
	Serafin
		LP: Columbia 33CX 1723-1724/
		    SAX 2316-2317
		LP: Columbia (Germany) C 91096-91097/
		    STC 91096-91097
		LP: Angel 3601
		LP: EMI 1C 163 00509-00510/
		    2C169 00509-00510/3C165 00509-00510
		CD: EMI CDS 747 4408/CDS 556 2842/
		    CMS 252 9432
		Excerpts
		LP: Columbia (Germany) C 80724/STC 80724
		LP: Angel 35831/36361/36933/36935/
		    36948/3696
		LP: EMI 1C 063 00772/SHZE 101/
		    1C 187 01398-01399/143 2631/
		    2C 059 43263
		CD: EMI CDC 252 9382/CDC 555 0162/
		    CDM 565 7472/CDS 754 1032/
		    CMS 565 7462/CMS 565 9522

Lucia di Lammermoor, Act 1 scene 2 and Act 2 scene 1

Naples March 1956 (24 March)	Borrelli, G.Raimondi, Panerai San Carlo Orchestra Molinari-Pradelli	CD: Myto MCD 90319 Video recording of these scenes may exist

Lucia di Lammermoor, excerpt (Regnava nel silenzio)

Athens August 1957	Athens Festival Orchestra Votto	LP: Timaclub MPV 6 CD: Hunt CD 537/CDHP 537 CD: Musica viva 88020 CD: Gala GL 316

Lucia di Lammermoor, excerpt (Il dolce suono/Ardon gl' incensi)

Turin February 1952	RAI Torino Orchestra De Fabritiis	LP: BJR Records BJR 143 LP: Timaclub 16 LP: Legendary Recordings LR 148 LP: Foyer FO 1007 CD: Foyer 2CF-2020 CD: Melodram MEL 26012 CD: Cetra CDC 5/CDMR 5001 CD: Rodolphe RPC 32484-32487 CD: Verona 27058-27059 CD: Hunt CD 536/CDHP 536
Mexico City June 1952 (14 June)	Bellas Artes Orchestra Picco	LP: Opera Dubs OD 101-2 CD: Eklipse EKR 33 CD: Memories HR 4581
Mexico City June 1952 (26 June)	Bellas Artes Orchestra Picco	CD: Memories HR 4581

Memories HR 4581 also contains the 2 performances of the Mad scene given in
Mexico City on 10 June 1952 (performance and encore - see complete recording
listed above)

Lucrezia Borgia, excerpt (Com' è bello!)

London November 1961	Philharmonia Tonini	CD: EMI CDC 754 4372

Paris
December
1963-
April 1964
	Conservatoire
	Orchestra
	Rescigno
		LP: Columbia 33CX 1923/SAX 2564
		LP: Columbia (Germany) STC 91410
		LP: Angel 36239
		LP: EMI 2C 069 00592/3C 065 00592/
		    2C 165 54178-54188/
		    1C 187 01398-01399
		CD: EMI CDC 747 2832/CDS 749 4532

Poliuto

Milan	Role of Paolina	LP: FWR 644
December	Corelli,	LP: BJR Records BJR 106
1960	Bastianini	LP: MRF Records MRF 31
	La Scala	LP: Replica RPL 2442-2444
	Orchestra & Chorus	LP: Foyer FO 1013
	Votto	CD: Hunt CD 520/CDHP 520
		CD: Melodram MEL 26006
		CD: Rodolphe RPC 32560
		CD: Verona 28003-28004
		CD: Virtuoso 269.7212
		Excerpts
		LP: Historical Recording Enterprises HRE 219
		LP: Gioielli della lirica GML 23
		LP: Dei della musica 14
		CD: Melodram MEL 16503
		CD: Foyer CDS 15003/CDS 15006
		CD: Memories HR 4400-4401
		CD: Palladio PD 4170
		CD: Hallmark 390362/311112

HENRI DUPARC (1848-1933)

L'invitation au voyage

Paris	Orchestre	Unpublished video recording
May 1965	National	May not have been preserved
	Prêtre	

Greater London Council
ROYAL FESTIVAL HALL
Director: John Denison, C.B.E.

S. A. GORLINSKY *presents*

MONDAY, NOVEMBER 26th and
SUNDAY, DECEMBER 2nd, 1973

An Evening with

MARIA CALLAS

and

GIUSEPPE DI STEFANO

At the piano:
IVOR NEWTON

S. A. GORLINSKY Ltd.
35 Dover Street, London, W.1.

The concert on November 26th is being recorded for television, to be shown on BBC2

Cover photo by Christian Steiner/E.M.I. Records

STEREO STC 91 359   und Mono

STEREO STC 91 246   und Mono

STEREO STC 91 155   und Mono

STEREO SMC 91 410   auch Mono abspielbar

STEREO SMC 91 385   auch Mono abspielbar

UMBERTO GIORDANO (1867-1948)

Andrea Chenier

Milan	Role of Maddalena	LP: Ed Smith UORC 286
January	Del Monaco,	LP: Opera Archives 1010
1955	Protti	LP: MRF Records MRF 66
	La Scala	LP: Cetra LO 38
	Orchestra & Chorus	LP: Melodram MEL 421
	Votto	CD: Melodram MEL 26002
		CD: Rodolphe RPC 232551-232552

Andrea Chenier, excerpt (La mamma morta)

Watford	Philharmonia	LP: Columbia 33CX 1231
September	Serafin	LP: Columbia (Germany) C 90409
1954		LP: Columbia (France) FCX 30088
		LP: Angel 35233
		LP: EMI 1C 053 01013M/3C 065 01013/
		2C 165 54178-54188/SLS 869/ASD 3824
		CD: EMI CDC 747 2822/CDC 555 0162/
		CDS 749 4532/CMS 565 7462/
		CMS 565 9522
		CD Single: EMI 881 2992

CHRISTOPH WILLIBALD GLUCK (1714-1787)

Alceste

| Milan
April 1954 | Role of Alceste
Gavarini,
Zampieri, Silveri,
Panerai
La Scala
Orchestra & Chorus
Giulini
Sung in Italian | LP: Ed Smith UORC 273
LP: Historical Operatic Treasures
 ERR 136
LP: Cetra LO 50
CD: Melodram MEL 26026
Excerpts
LP: Penzance PR 27
LP: Dei della musica 16 |

Alceste, excerpt (Divinités du Styx!)

| Paris
March-
April 1961 | Orchestre
National
Prêtre | LP: Columbia 33CX 1771/SAX 2410
LP: Columbia (Germany) C 91155/STC 91155
LP: Columbia (France) CVB 902
LP: Angel 35882/3743
LP: EMI 2C 069 00540/3C 065 00540/
 2C 165 54178-54188/SXLP 30166/
 143 3481/EMX 2123/ASD 4306
CD: EMI CDC 749 0592/CDC 555 0162/
 CDS 749 4532/CDS 754 1032/
 CMS 565 5342/CMS 565 7462/
 CDEMX 2123/CZS 252 6142
SAX 2410 also re-issued by Testament
as an audiophile LP edition |

Iphigénie en Tauride

| Milan
June 1957 | Role of Iphigénie
Cossotto,
Albanese,
Colzani, Dondi
La Scala
Orchestra & Chorus
Sanzogno
Sung in Italian | LP: FWR 649
LP: Penzance PR 12
LP: MRF Records MRF 63
LP: Morgan MOR 5704
LP: Cetra LO 54
CD: Melodram MEL 26012
Excerpts
LP: Dei della musica 16
CD: Melodram MEL 26026 |

Iphigénie en Tauride, excerpt (O malheureuse Iphigénie!)

Paris
May 1963
	Conservatoire
	Orchestra
	Prêtre
		LP: Columbia 33CX 1859/SAX 2503
		LP: Columbia (Germany) C 91246/STC 91246
		LP: Columbia (France) CVB 975
		LP: Angel 36147/3950
		LP: EMI 1C 065 00578/2C 060 00578/
		     3C 065 00578/2C 165 54178-54188
		CD: EMI CDC 749 0592/CDS 749 4532/
		     CMS 763 2442

Orphée et Euridice, excerpt (J'ai perdu mon Euridice!)

Paris
March–
April 1961
	Orchestre
	National
	Prêtre
		LP: Columbia 33CX 1771/SAX 2410
		LP: Columbia (Germany) C 91155/STC 91155
		LP: Columbia (France) CVB 902
		LP: Angel 35882
		LP: EMI 2C 069 00540/3C 065 00540/
		     2C 165 54178-54188/143 3481/ASD 4306
		CD: EMI CDC 749 0592/CDC 252 9382/
		     CDC 555 0162/CDS 749 4532/
		     CDS 754 1032/CMS 565 5342/
		     CMS 565 7462/CMS 565 9522/
		     CZS 252 6142
		SAX 2410 also re-issued by Testament
		as an audiophile LP edition

CHARLES GOUNOD (1818-1893)

Faust, excerpt (Il était un roi de Thulé/Ah, je ris!)

Paris
May 1963
	Conservatoire
	Orchestra
	Prêtre
		LP: Columbia 33CX 1858/SAX 2503
		LP: Columbia (Germany) C 91246/STC 91246
		LP: Columbia (France) CVB 975
		LP: Angel 36147/3742/3950
		LP: EMI 1C 065 00578/2C 069 00578/
		     2C 165 54178-54188/3C 065 00578/
		     1C 187 01398-01399
		CD: EMI CDC 749 0052/CDS 749 4532/
		     CDS 754 1032

Faust, excerpt (O nuit d'amour!)

Hamburg	Di Stefano	LP: TCC 501
October 1973	Newton, piano	CD: Eklipse EKR 33

Roméo et Juliette, excerpt (Je veux vivre dans cette rêve)

Paris	Orchestre	LP: Columbia 33CX 1771/SAX 2410
March–	National	LP: Columbia (Germany) C 91155/STC 91155
April 1961	Prêtre	LP: Columbia (France) CVB 902
		LP: Angel 35882/3950
		LP: EMI 2C 069 00540/3C 065 00540/
		2C 165 54178–54188/ASD 4306
		CD: EMI CDC 749 0592/CDC 754 7022/
		CDS 749 4532/CDS 754 1032/
		CMS 565 7462/CMS 565 9522
		SAX 2410 also re-issued by Testament
		as an audiophile LP edition

RUGGERO LEONCAVALLO (1858–1919)

I pagliacci

Milan	Role of Nedda	LP: Columbia 33CX 1211–1212
May–June	Di Stefano, Monti,	LP: Columbia (Germany) C 90396–90397
1954	Gobbi, Panerai	LP: Angel 3527/3528
	La Scala	LP: EMI 3C 163 00418–00419/SLS 819
	Orchestra & Chorus	CD: EMI CDS 747 9818/CDS 556 2872/
	Serafin	CMS 252 9432
		CD: NotaBlu 93.5152
		Excerpts
		45: Columbia SEL 1555
		LP: Columbia 33CX 1402
		LP: Columbia (Germany) C 80422/C 80689/
		C 70400/33WC 610
		LP: Angel 35345
		LP: EMI 1C 191 01593–01594M/SLS 5104/
		3C 063 00438
		CD: EMI CDC 555 2162/CMS 565 7462

PIETRO MASCAGNI (1863-1945)

Cavalleria rusticana

Milan
August 1953
	Role of Santuzza
	Canali, Ticozzi,
	Di Stefano,
	Panerai
	La Scala
	Orchestra & Chorus
	Serafin
		LP: Columbia 33CX 1182-1183
		LP: Columbia (Germany) 90380-90381
		LP: Angel 3509/3528
		LP: EMI 2C 163 00415-00416/SLS 819/
		    3C 165 00415-00416/EX 29 12693
		CD: EMI CDS 747 9818/CDS 556 2872/
		    CMS 252 9432
		CD: NotaBlu 93.5152
		Excerpts
		45: Columbia SEL 1549/SEL 1555/
		    SEL 1563/SEL 1567
		LP: Columbia 33CX 1402/33CX 1725
		LP: Columbia (Germany) C 80442
		LP: Angel 35345/36966
		LP: EMI 1C 061 00741/1C 063 00721/
		    1C 191 01433-01434M/3C 063 00438/
		    3C 063 00741/3C 065 17902/SLS 856
		CD: EMI CDC 754 7022/CMS 763 2442/
		    CMS 565 5342/CMS 565 7462/
		    CZS 252 6142

Cavalleria rusticana, excerpt (Voi lo sapete)

London November 1973	Newton, piano	LP: Ed Smith UORC 196 LP: MRF Records MRF 101 Also unpublished video recording
Amsterdam December 1973	Sutherland, piano	CD: Eklipse EKR 3
Brookville NY April 1974	Sutherland, piano	LP: Historical Recording Enterprises HRE 219 CD: Legato LCD 137
Tokyo October 1974	Sutherland, piano	LP: Historical Recording Enterprises HRE 323 CD: Cin CCCD 1037-1038 Also unpublished video recording
Montreal May 1974	Sutherland, piano	CD: Fonovox 78122

Cavalleria rusticana, excerpt (Tu qui, Santuzza!)

Hamburg October 1973	Di Stefano Newton, piano	LP: TCC 501 CD: Eklipse EKR 33
London November 1973	Di Stefano Newton, piano	LP: Ed Smith UORC 196 LP: MRF Records MRF 101 Also unpublished video recording
Amsterdam December 1973	Di Stefano Sutherland, piano	CD: Eklipse EKR 3
Brookville NY April 1974	Di Stefano Sutherland, piano	CD: Legato LCD 137
Tokyo October 1974	Di Stefano Sutherland, piano	LP: Historical Recording Enterprises HRE 323 CD: Cin CCCD 1037-1038 Also unpublished video recording
Montreal May 1974	Di Stefano Sutherland, piano	CD: Fonovox 78122

JULES MASSENET (1842–1912)

Le cid, excerpt (Pleurez, mes yeux!)

Paris March– April 1961	Orchestre National Prêtre	LP: Columbia 33CX 1771/SAX 2410
		LP: Columbia (Germany) C 91155/STC 91155
		LP: Columbia (France) CVB 902
		LP: Angel 35882/3950
		LP: EMI 2C 069 00540/3C 065 00540/
		      2C 165 54178–54188/143 3481/ASD 4306
		CD: EMI CDC 749 0592/CDS 749 4532/
		      CMS 565 5342/CZS 252 6142
		<u>SAX 2410 also re-issued by Testament</u>
		<u>as an audiophile LP edition</u>

London May 1961	Sargent, piano	LP: Penzance PR 15 CD: Legato LCD 162
London February 1962	Philharmonia Prêtre	LP: Opera Dubs OD 101-2 LP: Melodram MEL 674 CD: Melodram MEL 36513
Hamburg March 1962	NDR Orchestra Prêtre	LP: MRF Records MRF 83 LP: Voce 34 CD: Arkadia 4101 CD: Frequenz CMH 1 CD: Foyer CDS 15003/CDS 15006 CD: Laserlight 15224 CD: Great Opera Performances GOP 748 CD: Gala GL 322 CD: Hallmark 390362/311112 Laserdisc: Pioneer (Japan) PA 85-150 VHS Video: EMI MVD 491 7113

Manon, excerpt (Je marche sur tous les chemins)

Paris May 1963	Conservatoire Orchestra Prêtre	LP: Columbia 33CX 1858/SAX 2503 LP: Columbia (Germany) C 91246/STC 91246 LP: Columbia (France) CVB 975 LP: Angel 36147/3950 LP: EMI 1C 065 00578/2C 069 00578/ 2C 165 54178-54188/3C 065 00578 CD: EMI CDC 749 0592/CDS 749 4532

Manon, excerpt (Adieu, notre petite table)

Paris
May 1963
	Conservatoire
	Orchestra
	Prêtre
		LP: Columbia 33CX 1858/SAX 2503
		LP: Columbia (Germany) C 91246/STC 91246
		LP: Columbia (France) CVB 975
		LP: Angel 36147/3950
		LP: EMI 1C 065 00578/2C 069 00578/
		    2C 165 54178-54188/3C 065 00578/
		    SXLP 30166/EMX 2123
		CD: EMI CDC 749 0592/CDC 555 0162/
		    CDS 749 4532/CDS 754 1032/
		    CMS 565 5342/CMS 565 7462/
		    CMS 565 9522/CDEMX 2123/CZS 252 6142

Paris June 1963	Orchestre National Prêtre	CD: Melodram MEL 16502 CD: Virtuoso 269.7122 CD: Verona 27069 CD: Rodolphe RPC 32484-32487 CD: Gala GL 321 <u>Rodolphe incorrectly identified as Amsterdam 1959</u>

Paris
May 1965
	Orchestre
	National
	Prêtre
		LP: Opera viva JLT 4
		LP: Historical Recording Enterprises
		    HRE 334
		LP: Great Operatic Performances GFC 018
		CD: Melodram MEL 36513
		VHS Video: Bel Canto Society
		    BCS 0199
		<u>Televised performance</u>

Brookville NY April 1974	Sutherland, piano	CD: Legato LCD 137

Werther, excerpt (Air des lettres)

Paris
May 1963
	Conservatoire
	Orchestra
	Prêtre
		LP: Columbia 33CX 1858/SAX 2503
		LP: Columbia (Germany) C 91246/STC 91246
		LP: Columbia (France) CVB 975
		LP: Angel 36147/3950
		LP: EMI 1C 065 00578/2C 069 00578/
		    2C 165 54178-54188/3C 065 00578
		CD: EMI CDC 749 0052/CDC 749 5022/
		    CDS 749 4532/CDS 749 6002/
		    CMS 565 5342/CZS 252 6142

Paris June 1963	Orchestre National Prêtre	LP: Opera viva JLT 4 LP: Historical Recording Enterprises HRE 334 LP: Great Operatic Performances GFC 018 CD: Melodram MEL 16502 CD: Laserlight 15224 CD: Verona 27069 CD: Rodolphe RPC 32484-32487 CD: Gala GL 321 CD: Hallmark 390362/311102 Rodolphe and Hallmark incorrectly identified as Amsterdam 1959
Brookville NY April 1974	Sutherland, piano	CD: Legato LCD 137
Montreal May 1974	Sutherland, piano	CD: Fonovox 78122

GIACOMO MEYERBEER (1791-1864)

Le pardon de Ploermel (Dinorah), excerpt (Ombre légère)

Watford	Philharmonia	LP: Columbia 33CX 1231
September	Serafin	LP: Columbia (Germany) C 90409/C 90417
1954	Sung in Italian	LP: Columbia (France) FCX 30088
		LP: Angel 35233
		LP: EMI 1C 053 01013M/3C 065 01013/
		2C 165 54178-54188/ASD 2824/
		SLS 5018/SLS 5057
		CD: EMI CDC 747 2822/CDC 555 2162/
		CDM 565 7472/CDS 749 4532/
		CMS 565 5342/CMS 565 7462/
		CMS 565 9522/CZS 252 6142

San Remo	RAI Milano	LP: Historic Operatic Treasures ERR 134
December	Orchestra	LP: Opera viva JLT 1
1954	Simonetto	LP: Gemma WK 1001
	Sung in Italian	LP: Morgan A 006
		LP: BJR Records BJR 143
		LP: Timaclub 16
		LP: Legendary Recordings LR 148
		LP: Foyer FO 1007
		CD: Foyer 2CF-2020/CDS 15001/CDS 15006
		CD: Cetra CDC 5/CDMR 5002
		CD: Laserlight 15224
		CD: Verona 27058-27059
		CD: Hunt CD 536/CDHP 536
		CD: Newsound PNCD 0101
		CD: Great Opera Performances GOP 730
		CD: Gala GL 100.515
		CD: Hallmark 390362/311092

ROYAL FESTIVAL HALL

General Manager : T. E. BEAN, C.B.E.

WEDNESDAY, SEPTEMBER 23rd, 1959

S. A. GORLINSKY

presents

Maria Callas

LONDON SYMPHONY ORCHESTRA

(*Leader :* Hugh Maguire)

Conductor:

NICOLA RESCIGNO

PROGRAMME

Overture, Semiramide	*Rossini*
Tue che le vanità, from " Don Carlos "	*Verdi*
Intermezzo, Manon Lescaut	*Puccini*
The Mad Scene from " Hamlet "	*Thomas*

Ah, vos jeux . . . ;
Partagez-vous mes fleurs . . . ;
Et maintenant écoutez ma chanson.

INTERVAL

Overture, Le Maschere	*Mascagni*
Sleep Walking Scene from " Macbeth "	*Verdi*

Una macchia é qui tuttora.

Overture, Sicilian Vespers	*Verdi*
Final Scene from " Il Pirata "	*Bellini*

Oh ! s'io potessi . . . ;
Col sorriso d'innocenza
Oh, Sole ti vela . . .

S. A. GORLINSKY Ltd.
35 Dover Street, London, W.1

ROYAL FESTIVAL HALL

General Manager : T. E. Bean, C.B.E.

TUESDAY, FEBRUARY 27th, 1962

S. A. GORLINSKY

presents

Maria Callas

PHILHARMONIA ORCHESTRA

(*Leader*: Hugh Bean)

Conductor:

GEORGES PRÊTRE

PROGRAMME

Overture, Oberon	*Weber*
OBERON 'Ocean, thou mighty monster'	*Weber*
Overture, Semiramide	*Rossini*
LE CID 'Pleurez, mes yeux'	*Massenet*
LA CENERENTOLA 'Nacque all'affanno e al pianto'	*Rossini*

INTERVAL

Overture, Forza del Destino	*Verdi*
MACBETH 'La luce langue'	*Verdi*
DON CARLOS 'O don fatale'	*Verdi*
Carmen, Suite No. 2	*Bizet*
ANNA BOLENA Mad Scene and Finale, Act II	*Donizetti*

S. A. GORLINSKY Ltd.
35 Dover Street, London, W.1.

Front cover photograph by Angus McBean

WOLFGANG AMADEUS MOZART (1756-1791)

Don Giovanni, excerpt (Or sai chi l'onore)

Paris December 1963- January 1964	Conservatoire Orchestra Rescigno	LP: Columbia 33CX 1990/SAX 2540 LP: Columbia (Germany) C 91359/STC 91359 LP: Angel 36200 LP: World Records T 690/ST 690 LP: EMI 1C 053 01360/2C 069 01360/ 2C 165 54178-54188/3C 065 01360 CD: EMI CDC 749 0052/CDS 749 4532

Don Giovanni, excerpt (Non mi dir)

Florence January 1953	Maggio musicale Orchestra Serafin	LP: EMI EX 29 05983 CD: EMI CDC 754 4372/CDS 749 6002/ CMS 763 7502

Paris
December
1963-
January
1964
	Conservatoire
	Orchestra
	Rescigno
		LP: Columbia 33CX 1990/SAX 2540
		LP: Columbia (Germany) C 91359/STC 91359
		LP: Angel 36200
		LP: World Records T 690/ST 690
		LP: EMI 1C 053 01360/2C 069 01360/
		    2C 165 54178-54188/3C 065 01360
		CD: EMI CDC 749 0052/CDS 749 4532/
		    CDS 749 6002

Don Giovanni, excerpt (In quali eccessi!/Mi tradl!)

Paris
December
1963-
January
1964
	Conservatoire
	Orchestra
	Rescigno
		LP: Columbia 33CX 1990/SAX 2540
		LP: Columbia (Germany) C 91359/STC 91359
		LP: Angel 36200
		LP: World Records T 690/ST 690
		LP: EMI 1C 053 01360/2C 069 01360/
		    2C 165 54178-54188/3C 065 01360
		CD: EMI CDC 749 0052/CDC 754 7022/
		    CDS 749 4532/CMS 565 7462

Die Entführung aus dem Serail, excerpt (Martern aller Arten)

San Remo December 1954	RAI Milano Orchestra Simonetto Sung in Italian	LP: Historic Operatic Treasures ERR 134 LP: Opera viva JLT 1 LP: Gemma WK 1001 LP: Morgan A 006 LP: BJR Records BJR 143 LP: Timaclub 16 LP: Legendary Recordings LR 148 LP: Foyer FO 1007 CD: Foyer 2CF-2020/CDS 15001/CDS 15006 CD: Cetra CDC 5/CDMR 5002 CD: EMI CDC 754 4372 CD: Laserlight 15096 CD: Verona 27058-27059 CD: Rodolphe RPC 32484-32487 CD: Memories HR 4419-4420 CD: Hunt CD 536/CDHP 536 CD: Javelin HADCD 116 CD: Newsound PNCD 0101 CD: Great Opera Performances GOP 730 CD: Gala GL 100.515 CD: Hallmark 390362/311102
Dallas November 1957	Dallas Civic Opera Orchestra Rescigno Sung in Italian	LP: FWR 655 LP: Penzance PR 4/PR 15 LP: Historical Recording Enterprises HRE 232 LP: Collectors Limited Editions MDTP 028 LP: Paragon DSV 52014 CD: Great Opera Performances GOP 724 CD: Gala GL 323 CD: Verona 28007-28009 CD: Legato LCD 131 Rehearsal performance

Le nozze di Figaro, excerpt (Porgi amor)

Paris
December
1963-
January
1964
	Conservatoire
	Orchestra
	Rescigno
		LP: Columbia 33CX 1990/SAX 2540
		LP: Columbia (Germany) C 91359/STC 91359
		LP: Angel 36200/3743
		LP: World Records T 690/ST 690
		LP: EMI 1C 053 01360/2C 069 01360/
		    2C 165 54178-54188/3C 065 01360
		CD: EMI CDC 749 0052/CDM 565 7472/
		    CDS 749 4532/CMS 565 9522

AMILCARE PONCHIELLI (1834-1886)

La Gioconda

Turin September 1952	<u>Role of Gioconda</u> Barbieri, Poggi, Silveri, Neri RAI Torino Orchestra & Chorus Votto	LP: Cetra LPC 1241 LP: Turnabout THS 65051-65053 LP: DG LPM 18 164-18 166 LP: Everest S-419 LP: Eurodisc XR 71168 CD: Cetra CDC 9/CDO 8 CD: Palladio PD 4152-4154 Excerpts 45: DG EPL 30 130 45: Eurodisc CR 40634 LP: Cetra LPC 55041/LPS 12 LP: DG LPE 17 129 LP: Turnabout THS 65125 LP: Everest SDBR 3169/SDBR 7419 LP: Pickwick S 4048 CD: Cetra CDO 104 CD: Rodolphe RPC 32484-32487 CD: Foyer CDS 15001 CD: Laserlight 15224 CD: Palladio PD 4137 CD: Andromeda ANR 2518-2519 CD: Hallmark 390362/311092 CD: Fabbri GVS 03
Milan September 1959	Cossotto, Ferraro, Cappuccilli, Vinco La Scala Orchestra & Chorus Votto	LP: Columbia 33CX 1706-1708/ SAX 2359-2361 LP: Angel 3606/6031 LP: EMI 1C 153 00881-00883/ 2C163 00881-00883/3C163 00881-00883 CD: EMI CDS 749 5182/CDS 556 2912/ CMS 252 9432 Excerpts LP: Columbia (France) FCX 30161 LP: Angel 35940/36818/3743 LP: EMI 1C 061 00741/3C 063 00741/ 3C 063 01508/143 2631/2C 059 43263 CD: EMI CDC 754 7022/CMS 763 2442/ CMS 565 7462/CMS 565 9522

La Gioconda, excerpt (Suicidio!)

London November 1973	Newton, piano	LP: Ed Smith UORC 196 LP: MRF Records MRF 101 Also unpublished video recording
Amsterdam December 1973	Sutherland, piano	CD: Eklipse EKR 3
Brookville NY April 1974	Sutherland, piano	CD: Legato LCD 137
Tokyo October 1974	Sutherland, piano	CD: Cin CCCD 1037-1038 Also unpublished video recording
Montreal May 1974	Sutherland, piano	CD: Fonovox 78122

HEINRICH PROCH (1809-1878)

Deh torna mio ben!, air and variations

Turin March 1951	RAI Torino Orchestra Wolf-Ferrari	LP: Timaclub MPV 5 LP: Legendary Recordings LR 111 LP: Foyer FO 1007 LP: Historic Recording Enterprises HRE 7 CD: Foyer 2CF-2020 CD: Melodram MEL 36032 CD: Legato LCD 162 HRE 7 is actually a 7-inch disc playing at 33.1/3 rpm

GIACOMO PUCCINI (1858-1924)

La Bohème

Milan
August–
September
1956
	Role of Mimì
	Moffo, Di Stefano,
	Panerai, Zaccaria
	La Scala
	Orchestra & Chorus
	Votto
		LP: Columbia 33CX 1464-1465
		LP: Columbia (Germany) C 90553-90554
		LP: Angel 3560
		LP: EMI 1C 153 18182-18183/
		    2C163 18182-18183/3C163 18182-18183/
		    EX 29 09233
		CD: EMI CDS 747 4758/CDS 556 2952/
		    CMS 252 9432
		Excerpts
		LP: Columbia 33CX 1725
		LP: Columbia (Germany) C 80530/C 80689/
		    C 70400/33WC 610
		LP: Columbia (France) FCX 30149
		LP: Angel 35939/36940
		LP: EMI 1C 191 01433-01434M/
		    1C 191 01593-01594M/3C 063 01018/
		    3C 065 01480/SHZE 110
		CD: EMI CDM 769 5432/CDC 555 2162/
		    CDS 754 1032/CMS 565 5342/
		    CMS 565 7462/CZS 252 6142

La Bohème, excerpt (Sì, mi chiamano Mimì)

Watford
September
1954
	Philharmonia
	Serafin
		45: Columbia SEL 1546
		LP: Columbia 33CX 1204
		LP: Columbia (Germany) C 90392
		LP: Angel 35195
		LP: EMI 1C 053 00417M/2C 057 00417/
		    3C 065 00417/2C 165 54178-54188/
		    ALP 3799
		CD: EMI CDC 747 9662/CDC 754 7022/
		    CDS 749 4532/CDS 749 6002/
		    CMS 565 7462/CMS 565 9522

London October 1959	RPO Sargent	LP: BJR Records BJR 143 LP: Foyer FO 1007 CD: Foyer 2CF-2020/CDS 15003 CD: Legato LCD 162 CD: Melodram MEL 26034 CD: Great Opera Performances GOP 741 CD: Gala GL 316

La Bohème, excerpt (Donde lièta uscì)

Watford
September
1954
	Philharmonia
	Serafin
		LP: Columbia 33CX 1204
		LP: Columbia (Germany) C 90392
		LP: Angel 35195
		LP: EMI 1C 053 00417M/2C 057 00417/
		    3C 065 00417/2C 165 54178-54188/
		    ALP 3799/SLS 5057
		CD: EMI CDC 747 9662/CDC 555 0162/
		    CDM 565 7472/CDS 749 4532/
		    CMS 565 7462/CMS 565 9522

La Bohème, excerpt (Quando m'en vo)

Berlin May 1963	Deutsche Oper Orchestra Prêtre	LP: MRF Records MRF 83 LP: Historical Recording Enterprises HRE 7 CD: Eklipse EKR 33 HRE 7 is actually a 7-inch disc playing at 33.1/3 rpm
Stuttgart May 1963	SDR Orchestra Prêtre	LP: Voce 34 CD: Melodram MEL 26035 CD: Rodolphe RPC 32484-32487 Rodolphe incorrectly described as Amsterdam 1959
London May 1963	Philharmonia Prêtre	Unpublished private recording
Paris June 1963	Orchestre National Prêtre	LP: Opera viva JLT 1 LP: Historical Recording Enterprises HRE 334 LP: Great Operatic Performances GFC 018 CD: Melodram MEL 16502 CD: Verona 27069 CD: Gala GL 321

Gianni Schicchi, excerpt (O mio babbino caro)

Watford September 1954	Philharmonia Serafin	45: Columbia SEL 1546 LP: Columbia 33CX 1204 LP: Columbia (Germany) C 90392/C 90413 LP: Angel 35195 LP: EMI 1C 053 00417M/2C 057 00417/ 3C 065 00417/2C 165 54178-54188/ ALP 3799/SLS 5104 CD: EMI CDC 747 9662/CDC 754 7022/ CDM 565 7472/CDS 749 4532/ CMS 565 5342/CMS 565 7462/ CMS 565 9522/CZS 252 6142/ CDS 754 1032
Paris June 1963	Orchestre National Prêtre	LP: Opera viva JLT 4 LP: Historical Recording Enterprises HRE 334 LP: Great Operatic Performances GFC 018 CD: Virtuoso 269.7122 CD: Melodram MEL 16502 CD: Laserlight 15224 CD: Verona 27069 CD: Rodolphe RPC 32484-32487 CD: Hallmark 390362/311112 CD: Musica viva 88020 CD: Gala GL 316 Rodolphe, Hallmark and Musica viva versions incorrectly identified as Amsterdam 1959
Paris May 1965	Orchestre National Prêtre	CD: Melodram MEL 36513 VHS Video: Bel Canto Society BCS 0199 Televised performance
Hamburg October 1973	Newton, piano	LP: TCC 501 CD: Eklipse EKR 33
London November 1973	Newton, piano	LP: Ed Smith UORC 196 LP: MRF Records MRF 101 Also unpublished video recording
Amsterdam December 1973	Sutherland, piano	CD: Eklipse EKR 3
Brookville NY April 1974	Sutherland, piano	CD: Legato LCD 137
Tokyo October 1974	Sutherland, piano	LP: Historical Recording Enterprises HRE 263/HRE 323 CD: Cin CCCD 1037-1038 Also unpublished video recording

Unspecified version of the aria on CD Newsound PNCD 0101

Madama Butterfly

Milan
August
1955
	<u>Role of Butterfly</u>
	Danieli, Gedda,
	Ercolani,Borriello
	La Scala
	Orchestra & Chorus
	Karajan
		LP: Columbia 33CX 1296-1298
		LP: Columbia (Germany) C 90462-90464
		LP: Angel 3523
		LP: EMI 1C 153 00424-00426/
		   2C163 00424-00426/3C163 00424-00426/
		   SLS 5015/EX 29 12653
		CD: CDS 747 9598/CDS 556 2982/
		   CMS 252 9432
		<u>Excerpts</u>
		45: Columbia SEL 1617/SEL 1625/
		   SEL 1629/SEL 1637/SEL 1641
		LP: Columbia 33CX 1787
		LP: Columbia (Germany) C 80529/C 80689
		LP: Columbia (France) FCX 30135
		LP: EMI 3C 063 00550/SLS 5104/EX 29 01983
		CD: EMI CDC 749 5022/CDC 555 2162/
		   CDS 769 4002/CMS 763 2442/
		   CMS 764 4182/CMS 565 5342/
		   CMS 565 7462/CMS 565 9522/
		   CZS 252 6142

Madama Butterfly, excerpt (Un bel di)

New York April 1935	Unspecified accompaniment	LP: FWR 656 LP: Historical Recording Enterprises HRE 7 LP: Collectors Limited Editions MDP 016 CD: Eklipse EKR 33 <u>Callas sings (and is interviewed) under the name of Nina Foresti in this broadcast of the Major Bowes Amateur Hour; HRE 7 is a 7-inch disc playing at 33.1/3 rpm</u>

Watford
September
1954
	Philharmonia
	Serafin
		45: Columbia SEL 1546
		LP: Columbia 33CX 1204
		LP: Columbia (Germany) C 90392
		LP: Angel 35196
		LP: EMI 1C 053 00471M/2C 057 00417/
		   3C 065 00417/2C165 54178-54188/
		   ALP 3799
		CD: EMI CDC 747 9662/CDC 754 7022/
		   CDM 565 7472/CDS 749 4532/CMS565 7462

London September 1958	Orchestra Pritchard	LP: Voce 18 CD: Legato LCD 162 <u>Televised performance</u>

Madama Butterfly, excerpt (Con onor muore)

Watford
September
1954
	Philharmonia
	Serafin
		LP: Columbia 33CX 1204
		LP: Columbia (Germany) C 90392
		LP: Angel 35195/36930
		LP: EMI 1C 053 00417M/2C 057 00417/
		    3C 065 00417/2C165 54178-54188/
		    SLS 5057/ALP 3799
		CD: EMI CDC 747 9662/CDS 749 4532

Berlin May 1963	Deutsche Oper Orchestra Prêtre	LP: MRF Records MRF 83 LP: Historical Recording Enterprises HRE 219 CD: Eklipse EKR 33
Stuttgart May 1963	SDR Orchestra Prêtre	LP: Voce 34 CD: Foyer CDS 15003 CD: Melodram MEL 26035 CD: Rodolphe RPC 32484-32487 Rodolphe incorrectly identified as Amsterdam 1959
London May 1963	Philharmonia Prêtre	Unpublished private recording
Paris June 1963	Orchestre National Prêtre	LP: Opera viva JLT 4 LP: Historical Recording Enterprises HRE 334 LP: Great Operatic Performances GFC 018 CD: Virtuoso 269.7122 CD: Melodram MEL 16502 CD: Verona 27069 CD: Gala GL 321

Manon Lescaut

Milan
July 1957
	Role of Manon
	Di Stefano,
	Fioravanti,
	Calabrese
	La Scala
	Orchestra & Chorus
	Serafin
		LP: Columbia 33CX 1583-1585 .
		LP: Columbia (Germany) C 91033-91035
		LP: Angel 3654/6089
		LP: EMI 3C 163 00484-00486/RLS 737/
		    EX 29 00413
		CD: EMI CDS 747 3938/CDS 556 3012/
		    CMS 252 9432
		Excerpts
		LP: Angel 36966
		LP: EMI 1C 191 01433-01434M/
		    1C 191 01593-01594M/3C 065 01480/
		    SLS 856/SLS 5104
		CD: EMI CDC 555 0162/CDM 769 5432/
		    CDS 754 1032/CMS 565 5342/
		    CMS 565 7462/CMS 565 9522/
		    CZS 252 6142

Manon Lescaut, excerpt (In quelle trine morbide)

Watford
September
1954
	Philharmonia
	Serafin
		45: Columbia SEL 1546/SCD 2140
		LP: Columbia 33CX 1204
		LP: Columbia (Germany) C 90392
		LP: Angel 35195/36930
		LP: EMI 1C 053 00417M/2C 057 00417/
		    3C 065 00417/2C165 54178-54188/
		    ALP 3799
		CD: EMI CDC 747 9662/CDC 252 9382/
		    CDC 555 0162/CDM 565 7472/
		    CDS 749 4532/CMS 565 7462

Manon Lescaut, excerpt (Sola perduta abbandonata)

Watford
September
1954
	Philharmonia
	Serafin
		LP: Columbia 33CX 1204
		LP: Columbia (Germany) C 90392
		LP: Angel 35195/36930
		LP: EMI 1C 053 00417M/2C 057 00417/
		    3C 065 00417/2C 165 54178-54188/
		    ALP 3799/SLS 5057
		CD: EMI CDC 747 9662/CDS 749 4532

New York March 1974	Sutherland, piano	LP: Legendary Recordings LR 156

Suor Angelica, excerpt (Senza mamma)

Watford
September
1954
	Philharmonia
	Serafin
		LP: Columbia 33CX 1204
		LP: Columbia (Germany) C 90392
		LP: Angel 35195
		LP: EMI 1C 053 00417M/2C 057 00417/
		    3C 065 00417/2C 165 54178-54188/
		    ALP 3799
		CD: EMI CDC 747 9662/CDS 749 4532

Tosca

Mexico City June 1950	Role of Tosca Filippeschi, Weede Bellas Artes Orchestra & Chorus Mugnai	LP: Ed Smith UORC 184 LP: Historical Recording Enterprises HRE 211 CD: Melodram MEL 36032 CD: Legato SRO 820
Rio de Janeiro September 1951	Poggi, Silveri Teatro Municipal Orchestra & Chorus Votto	LP: Penzance PR 11 LP: Voce 34 CD: Melodram MEL 36032 Abridged recording but including large proportion of Tosca's role (one excerpt also on HRE LP 219)
Mexico City July 1952	Di Stefano, Campolonghi Bellas Artes Orchestra & Chorus Picco	LP: BJR Records BJR 153 LP: Morgan MOR 5201 LP: Cetra LO 41 CD: Melodram MEL 26028 CD: Great Opera Performances GOP 714 Excerpts LP: Legendary Recordings LR 112/LR 156 CD: Melodram MEL 26023 CD: Verona 28007-28009 CD: Memories HR 4372-4373 Some of these excerpts are dated June 1952
Milan August 1953	Di Stefano, Gobbi La Scala Orchestra & Chorus De Sabata	LP: Columbia 33CX 1094-1095 LP: Columbia (Germany) C 90325-90326 LP: Angel 3508 LP: EMI 1C 191 00410-00411/ 2C163 00410-00411/3C163 00410-00411/ SLS 825/EX 29 00393 CD: EMI CDS 747 1758/CDS 556 3042/ CMS 252 9432 Excerpts 45: Columbia SEL 1526/SEL 1530/ SEL 1543/SEL 1569 LP: Columbia 33CX 1725/33CX 1784/ 33CX 1893 LP: Columbia (Germany) C 80585/C 90413 LP: Angel 36940/36966 LP: EMI 1C 061 00741/1C191 01433-01434M/ 1C191 01593-01594M/3C 063 01015/ 3C 063 00741/3C 065 01480/SHZE 173/ SLS 856/SLS 5104 CD: EMI CDM 769 5432/CDS 754 1032/ CMS 763 2442/CMS 565 5342/ CMS 565 9522/CZS 252 6142 CMS 764 4182

Tosca/concluded

London January 1964	Cioni, Gobbi Covent Garden Orchestra & Chorus Cillario	LP: Limited Edition Society 107 LP: Great Operatic Performances GFC 008-009 CD: Melodram MEL 26011/IMC 203003 CD: Curcio-Hunt OPI 5 CD: Hunt CDMP 463 CD: Verona 27027-27028 CD: Virtuoso 269.7242 According to John Ardoin other performances in this series in January-February 1964 were probably recorded privately (see entry for Vissi d'arte below)

Paris
December
1964
	Bergonzi, Gobbi,
	Conservatoire
	Orchestra
	Opéra Chorus
	Prêtre
		LP: EMI AN 149-150/SAN 149-150/
		    CAN 149-150/SME 91403-91404//
		    1C165 00040-00041/2C165 00040-00041/
		    3C165 00040-00041/SLS 917
		CD: EMI CMS 769 9742
		Excerpts
		LP: EMI 1C 063 01965/2C 069 00316/
		    3C 065 00316/3C 965 01465/CVT 3561/
		    1C 187 01398-01399/SXLP 30166/
		    EMX 2123/143 2631/2C 059 43263
		LP: Angel 36326/3696/3863
		CD: EMI CDC 749 5002/CDC 252 9382/
		    CDC 754 7022/CMS 565 7462

Paris March 1965	Cioni, Gobbi Paris Opéra Orchestra & Chorus Rescigno	CD: Melodram MEL 26033 According to John Ardoin other performances in this series in February-March 1965 were probably recorded privately
New York March 1965 (19 March)	Corelli, Gobbi Metropolitan Opera Orchestra & Chorus Cleva	LP: Estro armonico EA 013 LP: Historical Recording Enterprises HRE 275 CD: Melodram MEL 26030
New York March 1965 (25 March)	Tucker, Gobbi Metropolitan Opera Orchestra & Chorus Cleva	LP: Historical Recording Enterprises HRE 306 CD: Melodram MEL 26035
London July 1965	Cioni, Gobbi Covent Garden Orchestra & Chorus Prêtre	LP: Voce 13 Abridged recording, but all of Tosca's role is included

Tosca, Act 2

New York November 1956	London Metropolitan Opera Orchestra Mitropoulos	LP: Voce 13 LP: Melodram MEL 079 LP: Great Operatic Performances GFC 008-009 CD: Hunt CD 537 CD: Melodram MEL 26011/MEL 36513 CD: Great Opera Performances GOP 714 CD: Musica viva 88020 VHS Video: Bel Canto Society BCS 0197 <u>Heavily abridged television performance</u> <u>omitting role of Cavaradossi; see also</u> <u>below under Vissi d'arte</u>
Paris September 1958	Lance, Gobbi Paris Opéra Orchestra & Chorus Sébastian	LP: Historic Operatic Treasures ERR 118 LP: Historical Recording Enterprises HRE 242 LP: Foyer FO 1006 CD: Foyer CDS 16010 CD: Rodolphe RPC 32495 CD: Gala GL 324 CD: Great Opera Performances GOP 748 Laserdisc: EMI LDB 991 2581 VHS Video: EMI MVD 991 2583 <u>Also issued on CD by Frequenz</u>
London February 1964	Cioni, Gobbi Covent Garden Orchestra & Chorus Cillario	Laserdisc: EMI LDB 491 2831 VHS Video: EMI MVD 491 2833 <u>Excerpts</u> VHS Video: Warner 0630 158983

Tosca, excerpt (Vissi d'arte)

New York November 1956	Metropolitan Opera Orchestra Mitropoulos	LP: Voce 13 LP: Melodram MEL 079 LP: Great Operatic Performances GFC 008-009 LP: Dei della musica 13 CD: Hunt CD 537 CD: Melodram MEL 26011/MEL 36513 CD: Memories HR 4293-4294 CD: Musica viva 88020
London June 1958	Orchestra Pritchard	LP: Legendary Recordings LR 111 CD: Legato LCD 162 <u>Televised performance</u>
Paris September 1958	Paris Opéra Orchestra Sébastian	LP: Historical Recording Enterprises HRE 263 CD: Melodram MEL 26020
London January or February 1964	Covent Garden Orchestra Cillario	LP: Historical Recording Enterprises HRE 219/HRE 232/HRE 263

TEATRO FILARMONICO DI VERONA

Palazzo dei Congressi

Sirmione

CONCERTO STRAORDINARIO

IN MEMORIA DI

Concerto straordinario

in memoria di

MARIA CALLAS

Maria Callas

DOMENICA 2 NOVEMBRE 1980

Ore 21

Martedì 16 Settembre 1980

Ore 21,00

Per te, Maria, a tutto ed a tutti ho rinunciato — um alla Mamma — ed a te, come sempre dicesti, tutto ho donato . . . . .

Titta

Inscribed photograph from Meneghini and concerts (opposite page) which he organised to commemorate the third anniversary of the death of Maria Callas

Turandot

Milan July 1957	Role of Turandot Schwarzkopf, Fernandi, Nessi, Zaccaria La Scala Orchestra & Chorus Serafin	LP: Columbia 33CX 1555-1557 LP: Columbia (Germany) C 90934-90936 LP: Angel 3571 LP: EMI 2C 163 00969-00971/ 3C 163 00969-00971/RLS 741/ EX 29 12673 CD: EMI CDS 747 9718/CDS 556 3072/ CMS 252 9432 Excerpts LP: Columbia 33CX 1792 LP: Columbia (Germany) C 80578 LP: EMI 3C 063 01019 CD: EMI CDC 749 5022/CMS 565 5342/ CZS 252 6142

Turandot, excerpt (In questa reggia)

Buenos Aires May 1949	Teatro Colon Orchestra Serafin	LP: Rodolphe RP 22413-22415 CD: Rodolphe RPC 22413-22415/ RPC 32484-32487 CD: Eklipse EKR 44 CD: Great Opera Performances GOP 778
Watford September 1954	Philharmonia Serafin	45: Columbia SEL 1533 LP: Columbia 33CX 1204 LP: Columbia (Germany) C 90392 LP: Angel 35195/36930 LP: EMI 1C 053 00417M/2C 057 00417/ 3C 065 00417/2C 165 54178-54188/ ALP 3799/SLS 5107 CD: EMI CDC 747 9662/CDC 754 7022/ CMS 565 9522/CDC 252 9382/ CDS 749 4532/CMS 565 7462/

Turandot, excerpt (O principe, che a lunghe carovane!..to end of Act 2)

Buenos Aires	Del Monaco	LP: Rodolphe RP 22413-22415
May 1949	Teatro Colon	CD: Rodolphe RPC 22413-22415
	Orchestra & Chorus	CD: Eklipse EKR 44
	Serafin	CD: Great Opera Performances GOP 778

Turandot, fragments from the duet Principessa di morte!

Buenos Aires	Del Monaco	LP: Legendary Recordings LR 111/LR 156
May 1949	Teatro Colon	CD: Eklipse EKR 44
	Orchestra & Chorus	CD: Great Opera Performances GOP 778
	Serafin	

Turandot, excerpt (Signore ascolta)

Watford	Philharmonia	45: Columbia SEL 1533
September	Serafin	LP: Columbia 33CX 1204
1954		LP: Columbia (Germany) C 90392
		LP: Angel 35195/36930
		LP: EMI 1C 053 00417M/2C 057 00417/
		3C 065 00417/2C 165 54178-54188/
		ALP 3799
		CD: EMI CDC 747 9662/CDC 555 2162/
		CDS 749 4532/CMS 565 6472/
		CMS 565 9522

Turandot, excerpt (Tu che di gel sei cinta)

Watford	Philharmonia	45: Columbia SEL 1533
September	Serafin	LP: Columbia 33CX 1204
1954		LP: Columbia (Germany) C 90392
		LP: Angel 35195/36930
		LP: EMI 1C 053 00417M/2C 057 00417/
		3C 065 00417/2C 165 54178-54188/
		ALP 3799
		CD: EMI CDC 747 9662/CDS 749 4532/
		CMS 565 9522

GIOACHINO ROSSINI (1792-1868)

Armida

Florence April 1952	Role of Armida Albanese, Ziliani, Salvarezza, Filippeschi, G.Raimondi Maggio musicale Orchestra & Chorus Serafin	LP: FWR 657 LP: Penzance Records PR 24 LP: Morgan MOR 5202 LP: Hope HOPE 224 LP: Collectors Limited Edition MDP 016/CLS 22030 LP: Cetra LO 39 CD: Great Opera Performances GOP 758 CD: Melodram MEL 26024 Excerpts LP: FWR 656 LP: Legendary Recordings LR 150 CD: Foyer CDS 15001

Armida, excerpt (D'amore al dolce impero)

San Remo December 1954	RAI Milano Orchestra Simonetto	LP: Historic Operatic Treasures ERR 134 LP: Ed Smith EJS 360 LP: BJR Records BJR 143 LP: MRF Records MRF 28 LP: Morgan A 006 LP: Timaclub 16 LP: EMI EX 769 7411 LP: Foyer FO 1007 CD: Foyer 2CF-2020/CDS 15001/CDS 15006 CD: EMI CDC 754 4372/CHS 769 7412 CD: Cetra CDC 5/CDMR 5002 CD: Melodram MEL 26024/MEL 26026 CD: Rodolphe RPC 32484-32487 CD: Verona 27058-27059 CD: Hunt CD 536/CDHP 536 CD: Great Opera Performances GOP 730 CD: Gala GL 100.515
Watford July 1960	Philharmonia Tonini	Columbia unpublished Recording incomplete

Il barbiere di Siviglia

Milan February 1956	Canali, Alva, Gobbi, Rossi-Lemeni La Scala Orchestra & Chorus Giulini	LP: Estro armonico EA 015 LP: MRF Records MRF 101 LP: Robin Hood RHR 507 LP: Cetra LO 34 LP: Melodram MEL 422 CD: Melodram MEL 26020 Excerpts LP: Limited Edition Society 100 LP: Historical Recording Enterprises HRE 219 LP: Dei della musica 5 CD: Melodram MEL 26026

London
February
1957
	Carturan, Alva,
	Gobbi, Zaccaria
	Chorus
	Philharmonia
	Galliera
		LP: Columbia 33CX 1507-1509/
		    SAX 2266-2268
		LP: Columbia (Germany) C 91030-91032/
		    STC 91030-91032
		LP: Columbia (France) 33FCX 760-762/
		    SAXF 120-122
		LP: Angel 3559
		LP: EMI 1C 165 00467-00469/
		    2C 167 00467-00469/SLS 853/
		    1C 197 00467-00469/EX 29 10933
		CD: EMI CDS 747 6348/CDS 556 3102/
		    CMS 252 7022
		Excerpts
		45: Columbia SEL 1658/SEL 1662/SEL 1687
		LP: Columbia 33CX 1790/SAX 2438
		LP: Columbia (Germany) C 80634/STC 80634
		LP: Columbia (France) FCX 30195
		LP: Angel 35936/36293/3696
		LP: EMI 1C063 00735/1C187 01398-01399/
		    2C 069 43284/3C 065 00552/
		    CVT 3195/SXLP 30166/SHZE 101/
		    EMX 2123/143 2631/2C 059 43263
		CD: EMI CDC 749 5022/CDC 555 5022/
		    CDC 252 9382/CDS 749 6002/
		    CDCFP 9013/CMS 565 5342/
		    CMS 565 7462/CZS 252 6142

Il barbiere di Siviglia, excerpt (Una voce poco fa)

Watford
September
1954
	Philharmonia
	Serafin
		45: Columbia (Germany) C 50556
		LP: Columbia 33CX 1231
		LP: Columbia (Germany) C 90409
		LP: Columbia (France) FCX 30088
		LP: Angel 35233
		LP: EMI 1C 053 01013M/3C 065 01013/
		   1C 148 31205/2C 165 54178-54188/
		   ASD 3824/SLS 5018/SLS 5104
		CD: EMI CDC 747 2822/CDC 754 7022/
		   CDS 749 4532/CMS 763 2442/
		   CMS 565 7462/CMS 565 9522
		CD: Javelin HADCD 116
		CD: Newsound PNCD 0101

London June 1958	Orchestra Pritchard	LP: Legendary Recordings LR 111 CD: Legato LCD 162 CD: Melodram MEL 16038 <u>Televised performance</u>
Paris December 1958	Paris Opéra Orchestra Sébastian	LP: Historic Operatic Treasures ERR 118 LP: BJR Records BJR 143 LP: Historical Recording Enterprises HRE 242 LP: Foyer FO 1006 CD: Foyer CDS 15003/CDS 16010 CD: Rodolphe RPC 32495 CD: Laserlight 15096 CD: Gala GL 324 CD: Memories HR 4293-4294 CD: Hallmark 390362/311102 CD: Great Opera Performances GOP 748 Laserdisc: EMI LDB 991 2581 VHS Video: EMI MVD 991 2583 <u>Also issued on CD by Frequenz</u>
Hamburg May 1959	NDR Orchestra Rescigno	LP: Historical Recording Enterprises HRE 228 LP: Rodolphe RP 12382 CD: Arkadia 4101 CD: Great Opera Performances GOP 748 CD: Gala GL 325 Laserdisc: Pioneer (Japan) PA85-150 VHS Video: EMI MVD 491 7113
Stuttgart May 1959	SDR Orchestra Rescigno	LP: Voce 18 CD: Eklipse EKR 37

La cenerentola, excerpt (Nacqui all' affano)

London November 1961– April 1962	Philharmonia Tonini	LP: EMI EL 749 4281 CD: EMI CDC 749 4282
London February 1962	Philharmonia Prêtre	LP: Opera Dubs OD 101-2 LP: Melodram MEL 674 CD: Foyer CDS 15009 CD: Rodolphe RPC 32484-32487 CD: Melodram MEL 36513 Foyer and Rodolphe incorrectly dated 1959
Hamburg March 1962	NDR Orchestra Prêtre	LP: Voce 34 CD: Hunt CDMP 410 CD: Great Opera Performances GOP 748 CD: Gala GL 322 Laserdisc: Pioneer (Japan) PA85-150 VHS Video: EMI MVD 491 7113
Paris June 1963	Orchestre National Prêtre	LP: Opera viva JLT 4 LP: Historical Recording Enterprises HRE 334 LP: Great Operatic Performances GFC 018 CD: Memories HR 4293-4294 CD: Gala GL 321 CD: Melodram MEL 16502/MEL 26024 CD: Virtuoso 269.7122 CD: Verona 27069

Paris
December
1963–
April 1964
	Conservatoire
	Orchestra
	Rescigno
		LP: Columbia 33CX 1923/SAX 2654
		LP: Columbia (Germany) STC 91410
		LP: Angel 36239/36933/3743
		LP: EMI 2C 069 00592/3C 065 00592/
		    2C 165 54178-54188
		CD: EMI CDC 749 0052/CDS 749 4532/
		    CDS 754 1032

Guillaume Tell, excerpt (Ils s'éloignent enfin/Sombre forêt)

London November 1961	Philharmonia Tonini Sung in Italian	LP: EMI EL 749 4281 CD: EMI CDC 749 4282
Paris December 1963– April 1964	Conservatoire Orchestra Rescigno Sung in Italian	LP: Columbia 33CX 1923/SAX 2564 LP: Columbia (Germany) STC 91410 LP: Angel 36239 LP: EMI 2C 069 00592/3C 065 00592/ 2C165 54178-54188/1C187 01398-01399 CD: EMI CDC 749 0052/CDS 749 4532

Il turco in Italia

Milan	Role of Fiorilla	LP: Columbia 33CX 1289-1291
August–	Gedda, Calabrese,	LP: Columbia (Germany) C 90455-90457
September	Rossi-Lemeni,	LP: Angel 3535/6095
1954	Stabile	LP: EMI 2C 163 03456-03457/SLS 5148
	La Scala	CD: EMI CDS 749 3442/CDS 556 3132/
	Orchestra & Chorus	CMS 252 9432
	Gavazzeni	Excerpts
		LP: Angel 3743
		CD: EMI CMS 763 2442/CMS 565 5342/
		CZS 252 6142

Semiramide, excerpt (Bel raggio lusinghier)

Milan September 1956	RAI Milano Orchestra Simonetto	LP: Opera viva JLT 1 LP: Gemma WK 1001 LP: Morgan A 006 LP: BJR Records BJR 143 LP: Timaclub 16 LP: Musidisc SCO 8221 LP: Melodram MEL 079 LP: Foyer FO 1007 CD: Foyer 2CF-2020/CDS 15002 CD: Cetra CDC 5 CD: Melodram MEL 26024/MEL 26026 CD: Laserlight 15096 CD: Rodolphe RPC 32484-32487 CD: Verona 27058-27059 CD: Hunt CD 537/CDHP 537 CD: Hallmark 390362/311092 CD: Great Opera Performances GOP 730 CD: Gala GL 100.515
Watford July 1960 and London November 1961	Philharmonia Tonini	LP: EMI EL 749 4281 CD: EMI CDC 749 4282
Berlin May 1963	Deutsche Oper Orchestra Prêtre	LP: MRF Records MRF 83 CD: Eklipse EKR 33
Stuttgart May 1963	SDR Orchestra Prêtre	LP: Voce 34 CD: Melodram MEL 26035 CD: Eklipse EKR 13
London May 1963	Philharmonia Prêtre	LP: Legendary Recordings LR 111
Paris June 1963	Orchestre National Prêtre	LP: Opera viva JLT 4 LP: Historical Operatic Enterprises HRE 334 LP: Great Operatic Performances GFC 018 CD: Melodram MEL 16502 CD: Verona 27069 CD: Memories HR 4293-4294 CD: Gala GL 321
Paris December 1963- April 1964	Conservatoire Orchestra Rescigno	LP: Columbia 33CX 1923/SAX 2564 LP: Columbia (Germany) STC 91410 LP: Angel 36239 LP: EMI 2C 069 00592/3C 065 00592/ 2C 165 54178-54188 CD: EMI CDC 749 0052/CDS 749 4532

Unspecified version of the aria on CD Javelin HADCD 116

CAMILLE SAINT-SAENS (1835-1921)

Samson et Dalila, excerpt (Printemps qui commence)

Paris	Orchestre	LP: Columbia 33CX 1771/SAX 2410
March–	National	LP: Columbia (Germany) C 91155/STC 91155
April 1961	Prêtre	LP: Columbia (France) CVB 902
		LP: Angel 35882/3950
		LP: EMI 2C 069 00540/3C 065 00540/
		2C 165 54178-54188/SXLP 30166/
		143 3481/EMX 2123/ASD 4306
		CD: EMI CDC 749 0592/CDC 555 0162/
		CDS 749 4532/CMS 565 5342/
		CMS 565 7462/CMS 565 9522/
		CZS 252 6142/CDEMX 2123
		SAX 2410 also re-issued by Testament
		as an audiophile LP edition

Samson et Dalila, excerpt (Amour! Viens aider ma faiblesse!)

Paris	Orchestre	LP: Columbia 33CX 1771/SAX 2410
March–	National	LP: Columbia (Germany) C 91155/STC 91155
April 1961	Prêtre	LP: Columbia (France) CVB 902
		LP: Angel 35882/3950
		LP: EMI 2C 069 00540/3C 065 00540/
		2C 165 54178-54188/ASD 4306
		CD: EMI CDC 749 0592/CDS 749 4532
		SAX 2410 also re-issued by Testament
		as an audiophile LP edition

Samson et Dalila, excerpt (Mon coeur s'ouvre à ta voix)

Paris	Orchestre	LP: EMI 2C 165 54178-54188/143 2631/
March–	National	2C 059 43263/ASD 4306
April 1961	Prêtre	LP: Angel 3950
		CD: EMI CDC 749 0592/CDC 754 7022/
		CDS 749 4532/CDS 754 1032/
		CMS 565 7462/CMS 565 9522

GASPARE SPONTINI (1774–1851)

La vestale

Milan December 1954	Role of Giulia Stignani, Corelli, Sordello, Rossi-Lemeni La Scala Orchestra & Chorus Votto	LP: Ed Smith UORC 217 LP: Historic Operatic Treasures ERR 117 LP: Cetra LO 33 LP: Melodram MEL 419 LP: Great Opera Performances GFC 54 CD: Melodram MEL 26008 CD: Great Opera Performances GOP 741 Excerpts LP: Dei della musica 16 CD: Fabbri GVS 03

La vestale, excerpt (O nume tutelar!)

Milan June 1955	La Scala Orchestra Serafin	LP: Columbia 33CX 1540
		LP: Columbia (Germany) C 80448
		LP: Angel 35304
		LP: EMI 1C 053 01016M/3C 065 01016/
		    2C 165 54178-54188/ASD 3535
		CD: EMI CDC 747 2822/CDC 555 0162/
		    CDS 749 4532/CMS 565 7462/
		    CMS 565 9522
		CD Single: EMI 881 2992

La vestale, excerpt (Caro oggetto)

Milan June 1955	La Scala Orchestra Serafin	LP: Columbia 33CX 1540 LP: Columbia (Germany) C 80448 LP: Angel 35304 LP: EMI 1C 053 01016M/3C 065 01016/ 2C 165 54178-54188/ASD 3535 CD: EMI CDC 747 2822/CDS 749 4532

PUBLIC PERFORMANCES 1952
DIGITAL REMASTERING
IIR 4381

MEMORIES

MARIA
CALLAS

Le 4 Pazzie
da Lucia di Lammermoor
di Città del Messico 1952
INCLUDING
TWO UNPUBLISHED
PERFORMANCES

GUIDO PICCO

Maria
Callas

IN CONCERT

The Rarest Material
1951-1961

As selected by
John Ardoin

LCD-162-1

LEGATO CLASSICS

La vestale, excerpt (Tu che invoco)

Milan June 1955	La Scala Orchestra Serafin	LP: Columbia 33CX 1540 LP: Columbia (Germany) C 80448 LP: Angel 35304 LP: EMI 1C 053 01016M/3C 065 01016/ 2C 165 54178-54188/ASD 3535 CD: EMI CDC 747 2822/CDS 749 4532/ CMS 763 2442/CMS 565 5342/ CZS 252 1642
Milan September 1956	RAI Milano Orchestra Simonetto	LP: Opera viva JLT 1 LP: Gemma WK 1001 LP: BJR Records BJR 143 LP: Morgan A 006 LP: Timaclub 16 LP: Foyer FO 1007 CD: Foyer 2CF-2020 CD: Cetra CDC 5/CDMR 5007 CD: Rodolphe RPC 32484-32487 CD: Verona 27058-27059 CD: Memories HR 4419-4420 CD: Hunt CD 536/CDHP 536 CD: Great Opera Performances GOP 730 CD: Gala GL 100.515
Hamburg May 1959	NDR Orchestra Rescigno	LP: Historical Recording Enterprises HRE 228 LP: Rodolphe RP 12382 CD: Arkadia 4101 CD: Frequenz CMH 1 CD: Virtuoso 269.7122 CD: Great Opera Performances GOP 748 CD: Gala GL 325 Laserdisc: Pioneer (Japan) PA85-150 VHS Video: EMI MVD 491 7113
Stuttgart May 1959	SDR Orchestra Rescigno	LP: Voce 18 CD: Eklipse EKR 37
Amsterdam July 1959	Concertgebouw Orchestra Rescigno	LP: Collectors Limited Editions RPCL 2056 LP: BJR Records BJR 103 LP: Voce 34 CD: Legato LCD 162 CD: Verona 27069

AMBROISE THOMAS (1811-1896)

Hamlet, excerpt (A vos jeux!)

Milan September 1956	RAI Milano Orchestra & Chorus Simonetto Sung in Italian	LP: Opera viva JLT 1 LP: Gemma WK 1001 LP: Morgan A 006 LP: BJR Records BJR 143 LP: Timaclub 16 LP: Melodram MEL 079 LP: Foyer FO 1007 CD: Foyer 2CF-2020 CD: Cetra CDC 5/CDMR 5007 CD: Rodolphe RPC 32484-32487 CD: Verona 27058-27059 CD: Hunt CD 537/CDHP 537 CD: Great Opera Performances GOP 730 CD: Gala GL 100.515
Athens August 1957	Athens Festival Orchestra Votto Sung in Italian	LP: Timaclub MPV 6 CD: Melodram MEL 36513 CD: Hunt CD 537/CDHP 537 CD: Musica viva 88020 CD: Gala GL 316 All versions include partial repeat of the aria as an encore

London
June 1958
	Philharmonia
	Orchestra & Chorus
	Rescigno
		LP: Columbia 33CX 1645/SAX 2320
		LP: Columbia (Germany) C 90413
		LP: Angel 35764/3743
		LP: EMI 2C 065 00784/3C 065 00784/
		     2C 165 54178-54188
		CD: EMI CDC 747 2832/CDS 749 4532/
		     CDS 754 1032/CMS 565 5342/
		     CZS 252 6142

Mignon, excerpt (Je suis Titania)

Turin March 1951	RAI Torino Orchestra Wolf-Ferrari Sung in Italian	LP: Legendary Recordings LR 111 Recording incomplete

Paris
March-
April 1961
	Orchestre
	National
	Prêtre
		LP: Columbia 33CX 1771/SAX 2410
		LP: Columbia(Germany) C 91155/STC 91155
		LP: Columbia (France) CVB 902
		LP: Angel 35882/36816/3950
		LP: EMI 2C 069 00540/3C 065 00540/
		     2C 165 54178-54188 /ASD 4306
		CD: EMI CDC 747 0592/CDC 555 0162/
		     CDS 749 4532/CMS 565 7462
		SAX 2410 also re-issued by Testament
		as an audiophile LP edition

GIUSEPPE VERDI (1813–1901)

Aida

Mexico City
May 1950
	Role of Aida
	Simionato, Baum,
	Weede, Ruffino,
	Moscona
	Bellas Artes
	Orchestra & Chorus
	Picco
		LP: Ed Smith UORC 200
		LP: Historical Recording Enterprises
		    HRE 310
		CD: Melodram MEL 26009
		Excerpts
		LP: FWR 656
		LP: Historical Recording Enterprises
		    HRE 219
		CD: Eklipse EKR 44

Mexico City July 1951	Dominguez, Del Monaco, Taddei, Ruffino, Silva Bellas Artes Orchestra & Chorus De Fabritiis	LP: MRF Records MRF 21 LP: BJR Records BJR 104/BJR 151 CD: Cetra CDE 1026 CD: Documents LV 951–952 CD: Melodram MEL 26015 CD: Legato SRO 508 CD: Virtuoso 269.9222 Excerpts LP: FWR 656 LP: Rodolphe RP 22413–22415 CD: Rodolphe RPC 22413–22415
London June 1953	Simionato Baum, Walters, Neri, Langdon Covent Garden Orchestra & Chorus Barbirolli	CD: Legato LCD 187 Excerpts (Act 3) LP: FWR 646 LP: Robin Hood RHR 500 CD: Eklipse EKR 14 CD: Melodram MEL 36513

Milan
August
1955
	Barbieri, Tucker,
	Gobbi, Zaccaria,
	Modesti
	La Scala
	Orchestra & Chorus
	Serafin
		LP: Columbia 33CX 1318–1320
		LP: Columbia (Germany) C 90475–90477
		LP: Angel 3525
		LP: EMI 1C 153 00429–00431M/
		    2C163 00429–00431/3C163 00429–00431/
		    SLS 5108/EX 29 09763
		CD: EMI CDS 749 0308/CDS 556 3162/
		    CMS 252 9432
		Excerpts
		LP: Columbia 33CX 1681
		LP: Columbia (Germany) C 80657
		LP: Columbia (France) FCX 30157
		LP: Angel 35759/35938
		LP: EMI 1C 053 01676M/3C 063 00596/
		    SLS 5104
		CD: Palladio PD 4182–4183
		CD: EMI CDC 555 2162/CMS 565 5342/
		    CMS 565 7462/CZS 252 6142

Aida, excerpt (Ritorna vincitor!)

Mexico City June 1950	Simionato, Baum, Weede, Ruffino Bellas Artes Orchestra Picco	LP: Opera Subs OD 101-2 <u>Extract begins at Alta cagion v'aduna</u>

Paris
February-
April 1964
	Conservatoire
	Orchestra
	Rescigno
		LP: EMI ASD 2791/1C 063 03253/
		    2C 069 03253/3C 065 03253/
		    2C 165 54178-54188
		LP: Angel 36582
		CD: EMI CDC 747 7302/CDC 555 0162/
		    CDS 749 4532/CMS 565 7462/
		    CMS 565 9522

Aida, excerpt (Fu la sorte)

Mexico June 1950	Baum Bellas Artes Orchestra Picco	LP: Opera Dubs OD 101-2

Aida, excerpt (O patria mia!)

Mexico City June 1950	Bellas Artes Orchestra Picco	LP: Opera Dubs OD 101-2

Aida, excerpt (Pur ti riveggo)

Rome October 1950	Picchi Rome Opera Orchestra Bellezza	LP: Timaclub MPV 3 LP: Historical Recording Enterprises CD: Melodram MEL 26019 CD: Great Opera Performances GOP 778
Paris June 1964	Corelli Paris Opéra Orchestra Prêtre	CD: EMI CDM 754 4372/CDC 252 9382/ CDS 754 1032 CD: Palladio PD 4170
London November- December 1972	Di Stefano LSO Almeida	Philips unpublished

ROYAL FESTIVAL HALL

General Manager: T. E. Bean, C.B.E.

FRIDAY, MAY 31st, 1963

S. A. GORLINSKY

presents

Maria Callas

PHILHARMONIA ORCHESTRA

(Leader: Hugh Bean)

Conductor:

GEORGES PRÊTRE

PROGRAMME

Overture, William Tell	*Rossini*
SEMIRAMIDE:	
'Bel raggio lusinghier', Act I	*Rossini*
Overture, Semiramide	*Rossini*
NORMA:	
'Casta Diva' and *cabaletta* ...	
'Ah! Bello a me ritorna', Act I	*Bellini*

INTERVAL

Overture, I Vespri Siciliani	*Verdi*
NABUCCO:	
Abigail's recitative and aria: 'Ben io t'invenni o fatal scritto' ...	
'Anch'io dischiuso un giorno', Act II	*Verdi*
Three Intermezzi:	
Cavalleria Rusticana	*Mascagni*
Pagliacci	*Leoncavallo*
Manon Lescaut	*Puccini*
LA BOHEME:	
Musetta's Waltz Song: 'Quando me'n vo, soletta per la via' ...	*Puccini*
MADAMA BUTTERFLY:	
Death of Butterfly: 'Con onor muore . . . tu, tu, piccolo Iddio!' ...	*Puccini*

S. A. GORLINSKY Ltd.
35 Dover Street. London. W.1.

Tuesday, 21st January, 1964

The 192nd performance at the Royal Opera House of

TOSCA

OPERA IN THREE ACTS

Words by GIUSEPPE GIACOSA *and* LUIGI ILLICA
based on the play by Victorien Sardou

Music by GIACOMO PUCCINI
(Property of G. Ricordi & Co.)

Conductor CARLO FELICE CILLARIO

New production by FRANCO ZEFFIRELLI

Scenery by RENZO MONGIARDINO

Costumes by MARCEL ESCOFFIER

Lighting by FRANCO ZEFFIRELLI *and* WILLIAM BUNDY

CESARE ANGELOTTI, an escaped political prisoner	VICTOR GODFREY
A SACRISTAN	ERIC GARRETT
MARIO CAVARADOSSI, a famous painter and republican	RENATO CIONI
FLORIA TOSCA, a famous singer	MARIA CALLAS
BARON SCARPIA, Chief of Police	TITO GOBBI
SPOLETTA, a Police Agent	ROBERT BOWMAN
SCIARRONE, a Police Officer	DENNIS WICKS
A SHEPHERD BOY	DAVID SELLAR
A GAOLER	EDGAR BONIFACE

Soldiers, Police Agents, Noble Ladies and Gentlemen, Citizens

Aida, excerpt (from end of O patria mia...to end of Act 3)

Rome October 1950	Stigani, Picchi, Falchi, Romani Rome Opera Orchestra Bellezza	LP: Timaclub MPV 3 LP: Historical Recording Enterprises HRE 262 CD: Great Opera Performances GOP 778 CD: Melodram MEL 26009 See also under entry above for Pur ti riveggo

Aida, excerpt (La fatal pietra sovra me si chiuse...to end of opera)

Mexico City June 1950	Simionato, Baum Bellas Artes Orchestra Picco	LP: Opera Dubs OD 101-2

Aroldo, excerpt (Ciel, ch'io respiri!/Salvami tu, gran Dio!)

Paris December 1963- February 1964	Conservatoire Orchestra Rescigno	LP: Columbia 33CX 1910/SAX 2550 LP: Columbia (Germany) SMC 91385 LP: Columbia (France) SAXF 1008 LP: Angel 36221 LP: EMI 2C181 53452-53453/3C 065 01020/ 2C 165 54178-54188 CD: EMI CDC 747 9432/CDS 749 4532

Aroldo, excerpt (O cielo! Dove son io?/Ah degli scanni eterei)

Paris December 1963- February 1964	Conservatoire Orchestra Rescigno	LP: Columbia 33CX 1910/SAX 2550 LP: Columbia (Germany) SMC 91385 LP: Columbia (France) SAXF 1008 LP: Angel 36221/36930 LP: EMI 2C181 53452-53453/3C065 01020/ 2C 165 54178-54188 CD: EMI CDC 747 9432/CDS 749 4532

Attila, excerpt (O nel fuggente nuvolo!)

Paris February– April 1964	Conservatoire Orchestra Rescigno	Columbia unpublished

Paris
February
1969
	Conservatoire
	Orchestra
	Rescigno
		LP: EMI ASD 2791/1C 063 03253/
		    2C 069 03253/3C 065 03253/
		    2C 165 54178–54188
		LP: Angel 36852
		LP: Timaclub MPV 5
		CD: EMI CDC 749 4282/CDS 749 4532
		According to John Ardoin some sections
		may have been spliced in from the 1964
		recording

Un ballo in maschera

| Milan
September
1956 | Role of Amelia
Barbieri,
Di Stefano, Gobbi
La Scala
Orchestra & Chorus
Votto | LP: Columbia 33CX 1472–1474
LP: Columbia (Germany) C 90558–90560
LP: Angel 3557/6087
LP: EMI 1C 153 17651–17653M/
    2C163 17651–17653/3C163 17651–17653/
    RLS 736/EX 29 09253
CD: EMI CDS 747 4988/CDS 556 3202/
    CMS 252 9432
Excerpts
LP: Columbia 33CX 1681
LP: Columbia (Germany) C 80621/C 80689
LP: Angel 36929/36940
LP: EMI 1C 053 18065M/3C 063 17919/
    3C 065 17902/1C 191 01433–01434M/
    1C 191 01593–01594M/SLS 856
CD: Palladio PD 4182–4183
CD: EMI CDM 769 5432/CMS 763 2442/
    CMS 565 5342/C7S 252 6142 |
| Milan
December
1957 | Simionato,
Di Stefano,
Bastianini
La Scala
Orchestra & Chorus
Gavazzeni | LP: MRF Records MRF 83
LP: Morgan MOR 5709
LP: BJR Records BJR 127
CD: Hunt CD 519 /CDHP 519
CD: Virtuoso 269.7412
Excerpts
LP: Ed Smith UORC 150
LP: Dei della musica 7
CD: Foyer CDS 15002/CDS 15004
CD: Melodram MEL 36020
CD: Myto MCD 89003
CD: Hallmark 390362/311102 |

Un ballo in maschera, excerpt (Ecco l'orrido campo!/Ma dall' arido stelo)

Turin March 1951	RAI Torino Orchestra Wolf-Ferrari	LP: Timaclub 16 LP: Legendary Recordings LR 111 <u>Orchestral introduction and recitative</u> <u>missing from the recording</u>

Paris
February-
April 1964
	Conservatoire
	Orchestra
	Rescigno
		LP: EMI ASD 2791/1C 063 03253/
		    2C 069 03253/3C 065 03253/
		    2C 165 54178-54188
		LP: Angel 36852
		CD: EMI CDC 747 7302/CDS 749 4532

Un ballo in maschera, excerpt (Morrò ma prima in grazia)

Paris
February-
April 1964
	Conservatoire
	Orchestra
	Rescigno
		LP: EMI ASD 3535/1C 069 01299/
		    2C 069 01299/3C 065 01299/
		    2C 165 54178-54188
		LP: Angel 37557
		CD: EMI CDC 747 9432/CDS 749 4532

Il corsaro, excerpt (Egli non rieda ancor/Non so le tetre immagini)

Paris
February
1969
	Conservatoire
	Orchestra
	Rescigno
		LP: EMI ASD 3535/1C 069 01299/
		    2C 069 01299/3C 065 01299/
		    2C 165 54178-54188
		LP: Angel 37557
		CD: EMI CDC 749 9432/CDS 749 4532

Il corsaro, excerpt (Ne sulla terra/Vola talor dal carcere)

Paris
February
1969
	Conservatoire
	Orchestra
	Rescigno
		LP: EMI ASD 3535/1C 069 01299/
		    2C 069 01299/3C 065 01299/
		    2C 165 54178-54188
		LP: Angel 37557
		CD: EMI CDC 749 9432/CDS 749 4532
		<u>Cabaletta from this recording</u>
		<u>remains unpublished</u>

Don Carlo, excerpt (Tu che la vanità)

London
September
1958
	Philharmonia
	Rescigno
		LP: Columbia 33CX 1628/SAX 2293
		LP: Angel 35763
		LP: EMI 2C 053 00865/3C 065 00865/
		    2C165 54178-54188/2C181 53452-53453/
		    SXLP 30166/EMX 2123/
		    1C 181 01398-01399
		CD: EMI CDC 747 7302/CDS 749 4532
		    CDEMX 2123

Hamburg May 1959	NDR Orchestra Rescigno	LP: Historical Recording Enterprises HRE 228 LP: Rodolphe RP 12382 CD: Rodolphe RPC 32484-32487 CD: Arkadia 4101 CD: Melodram MEL 36513 CD: Great Opera Performances GOP 748 CD: Gala GL 325 Laserdisc: Pioneer (Japan) PA85-150 VHS Video: EMI MVD 491 7113
Stuttgart May 1959	SDR Orchestra Rescigno	LP: Voce 18 CD: Eklipse EKR 37
Amsterdam July 1959	Concertgebouw Orchestra Rescigno	LP: BJR Records BJR 103 LP: Collectors Limited Editions RPCL 2056 LP: Voce 34 LP: Melodram MEL 079 CD: EMI CDC 749 4282
London May 1961	Sargent, piano	LP: Penzance PR 15 LP: Historical Recording Enterprises HRE 219 CD: Legato LCD 162 Final phrase missing from the recording
London November 1962	Covent Garden Orchestra Prêtre	LP: Historical Recording Enterprises HRE 219 CD: Foyer CDS 15003 CD: Verona 27058-27059 CD: Hallmark 390362/311092 Laserdisc: EMI LDB 491 2831 VHS Video: EMI MVD 491 2833
Tokyo October 1974	Sutherland, piano	CD: Cin CCCD 1037-1038 Also unpublished video recording

Unspecified version of the aria on CD Newsound PNCD 0101

Don Carlo, excerpt (Non pianger mia compagna)

Paris December 1963- February 1964	Conservatoire Orchestra Rescigno	LP: Columbia 33CX 1910/SAX 2550 LP: Columbia (Germany) SMC 91385 LP: Columbia (France) SAXF 1008 LP: Angel 36221 LP: EMI 3C 065 01020/ 2C165 54178-54188/2C181 53452-53453 CD: EMI CDC 747 9432/CDS 749 4532

Don Carlo, excerpt (Io vengo a domandar)

London November- December 1972	Di Stefano LSO Almeida	Philips unpublished
Hamburg October 1973	Di Stefano Newton, piano	LP: TCC 501 CD: Eklipse EKR 33
London November 1973	Di Stefano Newton, piano	LP: Ed Smith UORC 196 LP: MRF Records MRF 101 Also unpublished video recording
Amsterdam December 1973	Di Stefano Sutherland, piano	CD: Eklipse EKR 3
Brookville NY April 1974	Di Stefano Sutherland, piano	CD: Verona 28007-28009 CD: Legato LCD 137
Tokyo October 1974	Di Stefano Sutherland, piano	CD: Cin CCCD 1037-1038 Also unpublished video recording

Don Carlo, excerpt (O don fatale!)

Hamburg March 1962	NDR Orchestra Prêtre	LP: MRF Records MRF 83 LP: Voce 34 CD: Arkadia 4101 CD: Frequenz CMH 1 CD: Melodram MEL 36513 Laserdisc: Pioneer (Japan) PA85-150 VHS Video: EMI MVD 491 7113
London April 1962	Philharmonia Tonini	CD: EMI CDC 754 4372

Paris
December
1963–
February
1964
	Conservatoire
	Orchestra
	Rescigno
		LP: Columbia 33CX 1910/SAX 2550
		LP: Columbia (Germany) SMC 91385
		LP: Columbia (France) SAXF 1008
		LP: Angel 36221/3696
		LP: EMI 3C 065 01020/SHZE 101/
		    2C165 54178-54188/1C187 01398-01399/
		    2C181 53452-53453
		CD: EMI CDC 747 9432/CDC 555 0162/
		    CDC 252 9382/CDS 749 4532/
		    CMS 565 7462

Ernani, excerpt (Ernani, involami!)

London
September
1958
	Philharmonia
	Rescigno
		LP: Columbia 33CX 1628/SAX 2293
		LP: Angel 35763/3743
		LP: EMI 2C053 00865/2C181 53452-53453/
		    2C 165 54178-54188/3C 065 00865
		CD: EMI CDC 747 7302/CDC 555 0162/
		    CDS 749 4532/CMS 565 7462

Amsterdam July 1959	Concertgebouw Orchestra Rescigno	LP: BJR Records BJR 103 LP: Collectors Limited Editions RPCL 2056 LP: Voce 34 CD: Verona 27069 CD: Legato LCD 162
Hamburg March 1962	NDR Orchestra Prêtre	LP: Voce 34 CD: Arkadia 4101 CD: Virtuoso 269.7122 CD: Foyer CDS 15003 CD: Melodram MEL 36513 CD: Great Opera Performances GOP 748 CD: Gala GL 322 CD: Hallmark 390362/311102 Laserdisc: Pioneer (Japan) PA85-150 VHS Video: EMI MVD 491 7113

La forza del destino

Milan
August
1954
	Role of Leonora
	Nicolai, Tucker,
	Tagliabue,Capecchi,
	Rossi-Lemeni
	La Scala
	Orchestra & Chorus
	Serafin
		LP: Columbia 33CX 1259-1260
		LP: Columbia (Germany) C 90428-90430
		LP: Angel 3531/6088
		LP: EMI 1C 153 00966-00968M/
		    2C163 53016-53018/3C163 00966-00968/
		    SLS 5120/EX 29 09213
		CD: EMI CDS 747 5818/CDS 556 3232/
		    CMS 252 9432
		Excerpts
		45: Columbia SEL 1681
		LP: Columbia 33CX 1502/33CX 1681
		LP: Columbia (Germany) C 90417/C 80444
		LP: Angel 35432/35759
		LP: EMI 1C 053 01507M/3C 063 01507/
		    SLS 5104
		CD: Palladio PD 4182-4183
		CD: EMI CMS 565 5342/CZS 252 6142

La forza del destino, excerpt (Pace, pace, mio Dio!)

Athens August 1957	Athens Festival Orchestra Votto	LP: BJR Records BJR 143 LP: Timaclub MPV 6 LP: Musidisc SC 8221 LP: Foyer FO 1007 CD: Foyer 2CF-2020/CDS 15002 CD: Hunt CD 537/CDHP 537 CD: Melodram MEL 36513 CD: Gala GL 316 CD: Musica viva 88020

La forza del destino, excerpt (Madre, pietosa vergine)

Paris August 1977	Devetzi, piano	CD: Eklipse EKR 33 Fragmentary rehearsal recording

La forza del destino, excerpt (Ah per sempre!)

London November- December 1972	Di Stefano LSO Almeida	Philips unpublished
Hamburg October 1973	Di Stefano Newton, piano	CD: Eklipse EKR 33

I Lombardi, excerpt (Se vano è il pregare)

Paris
February–
April 1964
	Conservatoire
	Orchestra
	Rescigno
		LP: EMI ASD 2791/1C 063 03253/
		   2C 069 03253/3C 065 03253/
		   2C 165 54178-54188
		LP: Angel 36852
		CD: EMI CDC 747 7302/CDS 749 4532

I Lombardi, excerpt (Te vergin santa)

Paris February– April 1964	Conservatoire Orchestra Rescigno	Columbia unpublished

Paris
February
1969
	Conservatoire
	Orchestra
	Rescigno
		LP: EMI ASD 2791/1C 063 03253/
		   2C 069 03253/3C 065 03253/
		   2C 165 54178-54188
		LP: Angel 36852
		LP: Timaclub MPV 5
		CD: EMI CDC 749 4282/CDS 749 4532
		Some sections of the published
		recording are spliced in from
		the 1964 sessions

Macbeth

Milan December 1952	Role of Lady Macbeth Penno, Tajo, Mascherini La Scala Orchestra & Chorus De Sabata	LP: FWR 655 LP: Opera viva JLT 3 LP: Estro armonico EA 005 LP: BJR Records BJR 117 LP: MRF Records MRF 61 LP: Discocorp IGI 287 LP: Cetra LO 10 LP: Turnabout THS 65131-65133 LP: Columbia (Japan) GT 7056-7058 LP: Foyer FO 1016 CD: Movimento musica 051.022 CD: Nuova era NE 2202-2203 CD: Hunt CDLSMH 34027 CD: Legendary Recordings LRCD 1003 CD: EMI CMS 764 9442 CD: Great Opera Performances GOP 750 CD: Canale 539013-539014 Excerpts LP: Opera viva JLT 1 LP: Gemma WK 1001 LP: Gioielli della lirica GML 38 LP: Legendary Recordings LR 148/LR 157 LP: Dei della musica 9 CD: Opera italiana OPI 11 CD: Rodolphe RPC 32484-32487

Macbeth, excerpt (Vieni t' affretta!)

Turin February 1952	RAI Torino Orchestra De Fabritiis	LP: FWR 655 LP: Opera viva JLT 1 LP: Gemma WK 1001 LP: BJR Records BJR 143 LP: Morgan A 006 LP: Timaclub 16 LP: Historical Recording Enterprises HRE 219 LP: Legendary Recordings LR 148 LP: Foyer FO 1007 CD: Foyer 2CF-2020 CD: Cetra CDC 5/CDMR 5001 CD: Melodram MEL 36020 CD: Verona 27058-27059 CD: Hunt CD 536/CDHP 536 CD: Great Opera Performances GOP 730 CD: Gala GL 100.515
Dallas November 1957	Dallas Civic Opera Orchestra Rescigno	LP: FWR 655 LP: Penzance PR 4/PR 15 LP: Historical Recording Enterprises HRE 232 LP: Collectors Limited Editions MDTP 028 LP: Paragon DSV 52014 CD: Great Opera Performances GOP 724 CD: Gala GL 323 CD: Verona 28007-28009 CD: Legato LCD 131 <u>Rehearsal performance</u>

London
September
1958
	Philharmonia
	Rescigno
		45: Columbia SEL 1633
		LP: Columbia 33CX 1628/SAX 2293
		LP: Angel 35763
		LP: EMI 2C 053 00865/3C 065 00865/
		    2C165 54178-54188/2C181 53452-53453
		CD: EMI CDC 747 7302/CDS 749 4532/
		    CMS 565 9522

Hamburg May 1959	NDR Orchestra Rescigno	LP: Historical Recording Enterprises HRE 228 LP: Rodolphe RP 12382 CD: Arkadia 4101 CD: Frequenz CMH 1 CD: Foyer CDS 15003 CD: Virtuoso 269.7122 CD: Great Opera Performances GOP 748 CD: Gala GL 325 CD: Hallmark 390362/311112 Laserdisc: Pioneer (Japan) PA85-150 VHS Video: EMI MVD 491 7113
Stuttgart May 1959	SDR Orchestra Rescigno	LP: Voce 18 CD: Eklipse EKR 37

<u>Unspecified version of the aria on CD Newsound PNCD 0101</u>

Macbeth, excerpt (La luce langue)

London
September
1958
	Philharmonia
	Rescigno
		LP: Columbia 33CX 1628/SAX 2293
		LP: Angel 35763
		LP: EMI 2C 053 00865/3C 065 00865/
		    2C165 54178-54188/2C181 53452-53453/
		    1C147 30636-30637/SXLP 30166/
		    EMX 2123
		CD: EMI CDC 747 7302/CDS 747 4532/
		    CMS 565 5342/CZS 252 6142
		    CDEMX 2123

London February 1962	Philharmonia Prêtre	LP: Opera Dubs 101-2 LP: Melodram MEL 674 CD: Melodram MEL 36513 Recording incomplete

Macbeth, excerpt (Una macchia è qui tuttora)

London
September
1958
	Philharmonia
	Rescigno
		45: Columbia SEL 1633
		LP: Columbia 33CX 1628/SAX 2293
		LP: Columbia (Germany) C 70400/33WC 610
		LP: Angel 35763/36135/3696
		LP: EMI 2C 065 00865/3C 065 00865/
		    2C165 54178-54188/2C181 53452-53453/
		    1C187 01398-01399/ALP 2008/ASD 558
		CD: EMI CDC 747 7302/CDS 749 4532/
		    CMS 763 2442

London September 1959	LSO Rescigno	Unpublished amateur recording

Nabucco

Naples December 1949	Role of Abigaille Pini, Sinimberghi, Bechi, Neroni San Carlo Orchestra & Chorus Gui	LP: Cetra LO 16 CD: Melodram MEL 26029 CD: Documents LV 944-945 CD: Legendary Recordings LRCD 1005 CD: Canale 539001-539002 Excerpts LP: FWR 653 LP: Historic Operatic Treasures ERR 114 LP: Penzance PR 3 LP: Historical Recording Enterprises HRE 219 LP: Dei della musica 10

GIACOMO LAURI VOLPI

BURJASOT (Valencia - España) 16 - XI - 1977
Tel. 3 63 86 07

Egregio Comm. G. Meneghini,

Innanzitutto, permetta ch'io Le esprima le mie condoglianze
per la prematura scomparsa della Sua illustre Consorte,
alla quale Lei dedicò tempo, assistenza e dovizie perché
apprendesse il repertorio italiano, mettendole a fianco
un esperto della statura artistica del M°. Serafin: esperto assai costoso.
Senza di Lei, la Callas non avrebbe attinto le altezze
che in campo lirico, nonostante le ostilità del mondo
teatrale, potè raggiungere, lasciando traccia della sua
personalità nella storia del melodramma. Chi trionfò,
prima di addentrarsi nel bailamme della mondanità internazionale,
fu Maria Meneghini. Perché Maria Callas subentrò
quando già il miracolo era compiuto. L'Italia, non
la Grecia nè l'America, ha creato la creatura d'arte
alla quale tutti, oggi, rendiamo omaggio...
Senza Giov. Battista Meneghini, la Callas non sarebbe oggi,
Maria Callas...
Cordialmente la saluta

Giacomo Lauri Volpi

Tribute following the death of Maria Callas from colleague Giacomo Lauri Volpi

Nabucco, excerpt (Anch'io dischiuso)

Turin February 1952	RAI Torino Orchestra De Fabritiis	LP: BJR Records BJR 143 LP: Timaclub 16 LP: Legendary Recordings LR 149 LP: Foyer FO 1007 CD: Foyer 2CF-2020/CDS 15001 CD: Cetra CDC 5/CDMR 5001 CD: Rodolphe RPC 32484-32487 CD: Melodram MEL 36020 CD: Verona 27058-27059 CD: Hunt CD 536/CDHP 536 CD: Great Opera Performances 730 CD: Gala GL 100.515
London September 1958	Philharmonia Rescigno	LP: Columbia 33CX 1628/SAX 2293 LP: Angel 35763 LP: EMI 2C 053 00865/3C 065 00865 2C165 54178-54188/2C181 53452-53453 CD: EMI CDC 747 7302/CDS 749 4532
Berlin May 1963	Deutsche Oper Orchestra Prêtre	CD: Eklipse EKR 33
Stuttgart May 1963	SDR Orchestra Prêtre	LP: Voce 34 CD: Melodram MEL 26035 CD: Eklipse EKR 3/EKR 13
London May 1963	Philharmonia Prêtre	Unpublished private recording
Paris June 1963	Orchestre National Prêtre	LP: Opera viva JLT 4 LP: Historical Recording Enterprises HRE 334 LP: Great Operatic Performances GFC 018 CD: Melodram MEL 16502 CD: Verona 27069 CD: Laserlight 15224 CD: Memories HR 4293-4294 CD: Gala GL 321

Version of the aria on CD Hallmark 390362/311092/311102 incorrectly described
as with Concertgebouw Orchestra/Rescigno

Otello, excerpt (Salce, salce/Ave Maria)

Paris	Conservatoire	LP: Columbia 33CX 1910/SAX 2550
December	Orchestra	LP: Columbia (Germany) SMC 91385
1963-	Rescigno	LP: Columbia (France) SAXF 1008
February		LP: Angel 36221/3696
1964		LP: EMI 3C065 01020/1C187 01398-01399/
		2C165 54178-54188/2C181 53452-53453
		CD: EMI CDC 747 9432/CDS 749 4532/
		CDM 565 7472/CDS 754 1032/
		CMS 565 9522
		<u>565 7472, 754 1032 and 565 9522 contain</u>
		<u>only Ave Maria</u>

Otello, excerpt (Già nella notte)

London	Di Stefano	Philips unpublished
November-	LSO	
December	Almeida	
1972		

Rigoletto

Mexico City June 1952	Role of Gilda Garcia, Di Stefano, Campolonghi, Ruffino Bellas Artes Orchestra & Chorus Mugnai	LP: BJR Records BJR 101/BJR 149 LP: Cetra LO 37 LP: Melodram MEL 405 CD: Melodram MEL 26023 CD: Legendary LRCD 1006 Excerpts CD: Verona 28007-28009

Milan
September
1955
	Lazzarini,
	Di Stefano,
	Gobbi, Zaccaria
	La Scala
	Orchestra & Chorus
	Serafin
		LP: Columbia 33CX 1324-1326
		LP: Columbia (Germany) C 90481-90483
		LP: Angel 3537
		LP: EMI 1C 153 01346-01347M/
		    2C163 00432-00434/3C163 00432-00434/
		    2C163 03227-03229/SLS 5108/EX 29 09283
		CD: EMI CDS 747 4698/CDS 556 3272/
		    CMS 252 9432
		Excerpts
		45: Columbia SEL 1650/SEL 1656/
		    SEL 1659/SEL 1676
		45: Columbia (Germany) C 50556
		LP: Columbia 33CX 1582/33CX 1681
		LP: Columbia (Germany) C 70400/33WC 610/
		    C 80431/C 80689
		LP: Columbia (France) FCX 30155
		LP: Angel 35518/35759/36929/36940
		LP: EMI 1C053 00483M/1C191 01433-01434M/
		    3C 063 00483/3C 065 17902/SLS 856/
		    SLS 5057/SLS 5104
		CD: Palladio PD 4182-4184
		CD: EMI CDC 749 5022/CDC 754 7022/
		    CDC 252 9382/CDM 769 5432/
		    CMS 565 5342/CMS 565 7462/
		    CMS 565 9522/CZS 252 6142

La traviata

Mexico City July 1951	Role of Violetta Valletti, Taddei Bellas Artes Orchestra & Chorus De Fabritiis	LP: Historical Recording Enterprises HRE 220 CD: Melodram MEL 26019 Excerpts LP: FWR 650 LP: BJR Records BJR 130 LP: Rodolphe RP 22413-22415 CD: Rodolphe RPC 22413-22415
Mexico City June 1952	Di Stefano, Campolonghi Bellas Artes Orchestra & Chorus Mugnai	LP: Ed Smith UORC 181 LP: BJR Records BJR 130 CD: Melodram MEL 26021 CD: Rodolphe RPC 32431-32432 Excerpts LP: Legendary Recordings LR 112 CD: Rodolphe RPC 32484-32487 CD: Verona 28007-28009
Turin September 1953	Albanese, Savarese RAI Torino Orchestra & Chorus Santini	LP: Cetra LPC 1246 LP: Everest S-425 LP: World Records OC 115-117 LP: Eurodisc XR 70044 CD: Cetra CDC 2/CDO 9 CD: Andromeda ANR 2504-2505 CD: Bellaphon 693.22002 Excerpts 45: Eurodisc CR 40634 LP: Cetra LPC 55041/LPS 12 LP: Everest SDBR 3169/SDBR 3293/SDBR 7425 LP: Pickwick S-4051 LP: Turnabout THS 65125 LP: Eurodisc KR 70052 CD: Fabbri GVS 03 CD: Cetra CDC 5/CDO 104 CD: Palladio PD 4137/PD 4182-4183 CD: Andromeda ANR 2510-2519
Milan May 1955	Di Stefano, Bastianini La Scala Orchestra & Chorus Giulini	LP: MRF Records MRF 87 LP: Morgan MOR 5501 LP: Cetra LO 28 LP: Discocorp RR 474 LP: Columbia (Japan) GT 7051-7052 LP: Foyer FO 1003 CD: Foyer 2CF-2001 CD: Hunt CD 501/CDHP 501 CD: EMI CMS 763 6282 CD: Amplitude HRCDO 2-8501 Excerpts LP: Dei della musica 1 CD: Foyer CDS 15002/CDS 14004/CDS 15006 CD: Myto MCD 89003 CD: Memories HR 4372-4373/HR 4400-4401 CD: Hallmark 390362/311102

La traviata/concluded

Milan
January
1956
	G.Raimondi,
	Bastianini
	La Scala
	Orchestra & Chorus
	Giulini
		LP: Historical Recording Enterprises
		    HRE 272
		CD: Myto MCD 89003
		Excerpts
		LP: Historical Recording Enterprises
		    HRE 219
		LP: Dei della musica 1
		CD: Laserlight 15096
		CD: Hunt CD 501/CDHP 501

Lisbon
March 1958
	Kraus, Sereni
	San Carlos
	Orchestra & Chorus
	Ghione
		LP: Historical Recording Enterprises
		    HRE 277
		LP: Collectors Limited Editions
		    CLS 22013
		LP: Foyer FO 1003
		LP: Stradivarius 2301-2302
		LP: Movimento musica 02.002
		LP: EMI RLS 757/1C 157 03893-03894M/
		    2C 163 03893-03894
		CD: EMI CDS 749 1878/CDS 556 3302/
		    CMS 252 9432
		CD: Movimento musica 051.021
		Excerpts
		CD: Melodram MEL 36513/MEL 26007
		CD: EMI CDC 749 5022/CDC 754 7022/
		    CDC 555 0162/CMS 763 2442/
		    CMS 764 4182/CMS 565 7462
		VHS Video: Legato LCV 017
		VHS Video: Warner 0630 158983

London
June 1958
	Valletti, Zanasi
	Covent Garden
	Orchestra & Chorus
	Rescigno
		LP: FWR 652
		LP: Limited Editions Society LER 102
		LP: Collectors Limited Editions
		    AMDRL 22808
		CD: Replica (Japan) 54DC 831-832
		CD: Melodram MEL 26007
		CD: Documents LV 961-962
		CD: Hunt CDMP 465
		CD: Verona 27054-27055
		CD: Virtuoso 269.7292
		Excerpts
		LP: Historical Recording Enterprises
		    HRE 219
		LP: Musidisc SC 8221
		LP: Dei della musica 13
		LP: Foyer FO 1007
		LP: Paragon DSV 52014
		CD: Foyer 2CF-2020

La traviata, excerpt (Ah fors' è lui!/Sempre libera)

Dallas	Dallas Civic	LP: FWR 646
November	Opera Orchestra	LP: Historical Recording Enterprises
1957	Rescigno	HRE 232
		LP: Collectors Limited Editions MDTP 028
		CD: Melodram MEL 26016
		CD: Legato LCD 131
		CD: Verona 28007-28009
		CD: Great Opera Performances GOP 724
		CD: Gala GL 323
		Rehearsal performance

Il trovatore

Mexico City	Role of Leonora	LP: Historical Recording Enterprises
June 1950	Simionato, Baum,	CD: Melodram MEL 26017
(20 June)	Warren, Moscona	Excerpts
	Bellas Artes	LP: BJR Records BJR 102
	Orchestra & Chorus	LP: Rodolphe RP 22413-22415
	Picco	LP: Legendary Recordings LR 157
		CD: Rodolphe RPC 22413-22415
		For excerpts from another 1950 Mexico performance see below
Naples	Elmo, Lauri-Volpi,	LP: Ed Smith UORC 304
January	Silveri, Tajo	LP: FWR 654
1951	San Carlo	LP: Cetra LO 29
	Orchestra & Chorus	LP: Discocorp RR 473
	Serafin	CD: Melodram MEL 26001
		CD: Documents LV 948-949
		Excerpts
		LP: Historical Recording Enterprises HRE 219
		LP: Ed Smith ANNA 1040
Milan	Stignani, Penno,	LP: MRF Records MRF 78
February	Tagliabue,	LP: Robin Hood RHR 500
1953	Modesti	CD: Legendary Recordings LRCD 1007
	La Scala	CD: Myto MCD 90213
	Orchestra & Chorus	Excerpts
	Votto	LP: Historical Recording Enterprises HRE 219
		LP: Dei della musica 4
		CD: Foyer CDS 15001
		CD: Laserlight 15224
		CD: Hallmark 390362/311112

Il trovatore/concluded

Milan	Barbieri,	LP: Columbia 33CX 1483-1485
August	Di Stefano,	LP: Columbia (Germany) C 90561-90563
1956	Panerai, Zaccaria	LP: Angel 3554
	La Scala	LP: EMI 1C 153 00454-00456M/
	Orchestra & Chorus	2C163 00454-00456/3C163 00454-00456/
	Karajan	2C163 53750-53752/SLS 869
		CD: EMI CDS 749 3472/CDS 556 3332/
		CMS 252 9432
		Excerpts
		45: Columbia SEL 1641/SEL 1645/
		SEL 1653/SEL 1671/SEL 1689
		LP: Columbia 33CX 1682
		LP: Columbia (Germany) C 70400/
		33WC 610/C 80492
		LP: Columbia (France) FCX 30181
		LP: Angel 36966/3743
		LP: EMI 1C053 01677M/1C191 01433-01434M/
		1C 191 01593-01594M/1C 061 00741/
		3C 063 00494/3C 063 00741/SLS 5104/
		3C 065 17902/SLS 856/SLS 5057/
		CD: EMI CDC 555 2162/CDM 565 7472/
		CDM 763 5572/CDM 769 5432/
		CDS 754 1032/CMS 565 5342/
		CMS 565 7462/CMS 763 2442/
		CZS 252 6142

**Il trovatore, excerpts (Oh! Leonora, tu desta sei/Qual voce!..to end of Act 1;
Udiste? Come albeggi, la scure al figlio/Non respingermi!..to end of opera)**

Mexico City	Simionato, Baum,	LP: FWR 651
June 1950	Petroff	CD: Eklipse EKR 14
(27 June)	Bellas Artes	Selection includes other items
	Orchestra	without Callas
	Picco	

Il trovatore, excerpt (Tacea la notte placida)

Mexico City June 1950 (27 June)	Bellas Artes Orchestra Picco	LP: FWR 651 CD: Eklipse EKR 14

Paris
February–
April 1964
	Conservatoire
	Orchestra
	Rescigno
		LP: EMI ASD 3535/1C 069 01299/
		    2C 069 01299/3C 065 01299/
		    2C 165 54178-54188
		CD: EMI CDC 754 9432/CDS 749 4532

Il trovatore, excerpt (D'amor sull' ali rosee)

Athens August 1957	Athens Festival Orchestra Votto	LP: Timaclub MPV 6 CD: Hunt CD 537/CDHP 537 CD: Melodram MEL 16038 CD: Musica viva 88020 CD: Gala GL 316 Melodram incorrectly identified as London 1958
Paris December 1958	Lance Paris Opéra Orchestra & Chorus Sébastian	LP: Historic Operatic Treasures ERR 118 LP: Historical Recording Enterprises HRE 242/HRE 263 LP: Foyer FO 1006 CD: Foyer 2CF-2020/CDS 16010 CD: Rodolphe RPC 32495 CD: Melodram MEL 26001 CD: Gala GL 324 CD: Great Opera Performances GOP 748 Laserdisc: EMI LDB 991 2581 VHS Video: EMI MVD 991 2583 This version continues into the ensuing Miserere; also issued on CD by Frequenz

Paris
February–
April 1964
	Conservatoire
	Orchestra
	Rescigno
		LP: EMI ASD 3535/1C 069 01299/
		    2C 069 01299/3C 065 01299/
		    2C 165 54178-54188
		CD: EMI CDC 754 4372/CDS 749 4532

I vespri siciliani

Florence	Role of Elena	LP: FWR 645
May 1951	Kokolios-Bardi,	LP: Penzance PR 6
	Mascherini,	LP: MRF Records MRF 46
	Christoff	LP: Cetra LO 5
	Maggio musicale	LP: Melodram MEL 420
	Orchestra & Chorus	CD: Melodram MEL 36020/IMC 203003
	Kleiber	CD: Legendary Recordings LRCD 1008
		Excerpts
		LP: Dei della musica 17

I vespri siciliani, excerpt (Mercè dilette amiche!)

Watford	Philharmonia	LP: Columbia 33CX 1231
September	Serafin	LP: Columbia (Germany) C 90409
1954		LP: Columbia (France) FCX 30088
		LP: Angel 35233
		LP: EMI 1C 053 01013M/3C 065 01013/
		2C 165 54178-54188/ASD 3824
		CD: EMI CDC 747 2822/CDC 555 0162/
		CDS 749 4532/CMS 763 2442/
		CMS 565 7462

I vespri siciliani, excerpt (Arrigo! Ah parli a un cor)

Watford July 1960	Philharmonia Tonini	Columbia unpublished
Paris February– April 1964	Conservatoire Orchestra Rescigno	Columbia unpublished

Paris
February
1969
	Conservatoire
	Orchestra
	Rescigno
		LP: EMI ASD 2791/1C 063 03253/
		    2C 069 03253/3C 065 03253/
		    2C 165 54178-54188
		LP: Timaclub MPV 5
		LP: Angel 36852
		CD: EMI CDC 749 4282/CDS 749 4532/
		    CMS 565 5342/CZS 252 6142
		According to John Ardoin some sections
		may have been spliced in from the 1964
		recording

I vespri siciliani, excerpt (Quale o prode!)

London November– December 1972	Di Stefano LSO Almeida	Philips unpublished
London November 1973	Di Stefano Newton, piano	LP: Ed Smith UORC 196 LP: MRF Records MRF 101 Also unpublished video recording
Amsterdam December 1973	Di Stefano Sutherland, piano	CD: Eklipse EKR 3
Tokyo October 1974	Di Stefano Sutherland, piano	CD: Cin CCCD 1037-1038 Also unpublished video recording
Montreal May 1974	Di Stefano Sutherland, piano	CD: Fonovox 78122

RICHARD WAGNER (1813-1883)

Parsifal

Rome November 1950	Role of Kundry Baldelli, Christoff, Panerai, Modesti RAI Roma Orchestra & Chorus Gui Sung in Italian	LP: MCW 101/FWR 648 LP: Estro armonico EA 055 LP: Cetra LAR 41 LP: Foyer FO 1002 CD: Cetra CDAR 2020 CD: Melodram MEL 36041 CD: Virtuoso 269.9232 CD: Verona 27085-27087 Excerpts LP: Penzance PR 10 LP: Rococo 5369 CD: Melodram MEL 36513 CD: Great Opera Performances GOP 778 CD: Gala GL 320

Tristan und Isolde, excerpt (Mild und leise)

Turin November 1949	RAI Torino Orchestra Basile Sung in Italian	78: Cetra CB 20481/Parlophone CB 20481 LP: Cetra LPC 50175/LPC 55057 LP: OASI 532 LP: Morgan A 006 LP: Everest SDBR 3259 LP: Ember GVC 16 LP: Turnabout THS 65125 CD: Cetra CDC 5/CDO 104 CD: Foyer CDS 15001 CD: Rodolphe RPC 32484-32487 CD: Palladio PD 4137 CD: Verona 27058-27059 CD: Andromeda ANR 2518-2519 CD: Newsound PNCD 0101 CD: Fabbri GVS 03 CD: Great Opera Performances GOP 730 CD: Gala GL 100.515
Athens August 1957	Athens Festival Orchestra Votto Sung in Italian	LP: BJR Records BJR 143 LP: Timaclub MPV 6 LP: Legendary Recordings LR 151 CD: Hunt CD 537 CD: Melodram MEL 36513 CD: Musica viva 88020 CD: Gala GL 316

CARL MARIA VON WEBER (1786–1826)

Oberon, excerpt (Ocean, thou mighty monster!)

London February 1962	Philharmonia Prêtre	LP: Opera Dubs OD 101-2 LP: Melodram MEL 674 CD: Melodram MEL 36513
London April 1962	Philharmonia Tonini	CD: EMI CDC 754 4372
Paris December 1963– January 1964	Conservatoire Orchestra Rescigno	LP: Columbia 33CX 1990/SAX 2540 LP: Columbia (Germany) C 91359/STC 91359 LP: Angel 36200 LP: EMI 1C 053 01360/2C 069 01360/ 3C 065 01360/2C 165 54178-54188 CD: EMI CDC 754 4372/CDS 749 4532

Der Freischütz, excerpt (Leise, leise)

Turin March 1951	RAI Torino Orchestra Wolf-Ferrari Sung in Italian	Unpublished radio broadcast Tape may have been erased or lost

MISCELLANEOUS AND INTERVIEWS

Intervista a Maria Callas effetuata da Guido Oddo in occasione della prima recita della Vestale

Milan
December
1954

CD: Fabbri GVS 03

The Harewood Interviews

Paris
April 1968

VHS Video: Bel Canto Society BCS 0199
Excerpts
LP: Historical Recording Enterprises
    HRE 263
LP: IGS 001
CD: Gala 100.523
In-depth discussion of her artistic
development and detailed analysis of
her approach to the major roles in her
stage career; last shown on BBC 2 under
the title The Callas Conversations in
December 1993 and January 1994

Une interview de Maria Callas par Jacques Bourgeois

Paris
September
1968

45: EMI EPM 7
Disc included in an anthology of Callas'
recordings issued by EMI France under
catalogue number OVB 2171-2174

The Edward Downes Interviews

New York
December
1967-
January
1968

LP: Angel 3743/36622
CD: EMI CDM 565 8222/CMS 565 7462
Lengthy discussion of matters relating
to technique and interpretation
recorded for Metropolitan Opera
intermission broadcasts

Miscellaneous and interviews/continued

The David Frost Show

New York
December
1970

CD: Verona 28007-28009
90-minute discussion of the early years,
the singer's approach to her roles,
relations with the press, and problems
in her personal life; also unpublished
video recording

The Juilliard Master Classes

New York   Kohn, piano
November
1971-
March 1973

LP: EMI EX 749 6001
CD: EMI CDS 749 6002
Excerpts
LP: IGS 92/IGS 99
LP: Timaclub MPV 5
Callas coaches students in roles from
Don Giovanni, Fidelio, Medea, Norma,
Il barbiere di Siviglia, Rigoletto,
Don Carlo, Werther, La Bohème and
Madama Butterfly; the classes are
interspersed with extracts from Callas'
own recordings of the arias concerned

Callas: a documentary film

New York
December
1978

Unpublished video recording
LP: Historical Recording Enterprises
    HRE 263
WNET-TV documentary written by John
Ardoin and produced by Peter Weinberg,
containing interviews with prominent
colleagues and illustrated with many
sound and filmed recordings

Interviews recueillies par Alain Lanceron en hommage à Maria Callas

Paris
1978

LP: EMI PM 52 788
LP record of interviews in tribute to
Callas following her death in 1977: LP
included with the EMI France LP edition
Ses Récitals (2C 165 54178-54188)

Miscellaneous and interviews/concluded

Maria Callas: Vissi d'arte

Paris	Unpublished video recording
1979	RTF documentary film by Brigette Corea and Alain Ferrari containing many interviews and performance film

Callas: Life and Art

1987	Laserdisc: EMI LDB 991 1511
	VHS Video: EMI MVN 991 1512
	Documentary film produced by Picture Music International and directed by Jo Lustig

Maria Callas: South Bank Special

London	VHS Video: Polygram 079 2183
1987	Laserdisc: Pioneer (Japan) PA91-340
	A Tony Palmer documentary

Callas in her own words

	CD: Eklipse EKR 14
	Radio documentary from KUSC/Los Angeles, written by John Ardoin and narrated by Michael Wager

Callas reveals herself

1974	VHS Video: Bel Canto Society BCS 0197
	Mainly a Callas interview, but additional material contributed by other sources

Important note
The material listed here comprises most of the published documentary matter dealing with the life and career. It should, however, be emphasised that there exists a further quantity of sound and film footage: some of this is important, whilst other items are of a more trivial nature, dealing with dieting, professional rivalries and personal problems which do not necessarily have a bearing on the artistic legacy of Maria Callas.

MARIA CALLAS AS FILM ACTRESS

Medea: a film by Pier Paolo Pasolini

June-July
1969

VHS Video: Video Artists International VAI 17
Produced by Franco Rosselini and directed by
Pasolini, the film also featured Margareth
Clementi, Giuseppe Gentile, Massimo Girotti
and Laurent Terzieff. As far as could be
ascertained, Callas' speaking voice is heard
only in the Italian version and not in the
dubbings into other languages.

Magda Olivero
born 1910

Discography compiled
by John Hunt

MICHELE ACCORINTI

O salutaris hostia

Solda	Montanari, organ	LP: Great Opera Performances GOP 46
August 1981		CD: Great Opera Performances GOP 795

ADOLPHE ADAM (1803-1856)

Cantique de Noël

Details not confirmed	LP: Timaclub 21

FRANCO ALFANO (1875-1954)

Risurrezione

Turin	<u>Role of Katiusha</u>	LP: Historical Recording Enterprises
October 1971	Di Stasio, Condò,	HRE 237
	Gismondo, Stefanoni	CD: Legato SRO 839
	RAI Torino	
	Orchestra & Chorus	
	Boncompagni	

Risurrezione, excerpt (Dio pietoso)

Turin	RAI Torino	78: Cetra BB 25277
1949-1950	Orchestra	LP: Cetra LPC 55011/LPO 2041
	Simonetto	CD: Palladio PD 4162
		CD: Fabbri GVS 06
		<u>This recording also used as soundtrack</u>
		<u>for a TV performance now published on</u>
		<u>VHS Video by Bel Canto Society BCS 0115</u>
Amsterdam	Netherlands RO	LP: Collectors Limited Edition MDP 021
October 1962	Vernizzi	CD: Great Opera Performances GOP 709
		CD: Fanclub 101

JOHANN SEBASTIAN BACH (1685-1750)

O Haupt voll Blut und Wunden (Matthäus-Passion), arrangement
Also incorrectly described as Bist du bei mir

Milan	Catena, organ	LP: Ariston CLAR 13009
June 1970	Sung in Italian	LP: Oscar OSA 148
Solda	Montanari, organ	LP: Great Opera Performances GOP 46
December 1970	Sung in Italian	CD: Great Opera Performances GOP 795

BAUDISSONE

Ave Maria; Padre nostro

Milan	Bottesini Double	CD: Bongiovanni GB 55542
March 1994	Bass Quartet	
	Ranfaldi, violin	

LUDWIG VAN BEETHOVEN (1770-1827)

Liebe des Nächsten; Gottes Macht und Vorsehung (Gellert-Lieder)

Solda	Montanari, organ	LP: Great Opera Performances GOP 46
August 1971	Sung in Italian	CD: Great Opera Performances GOP 795

VINCENZO BELLINI (1801-1835)

I Capuleti ed i Montecchi, excerpt (Oh quante volte!)

New York October 1979	Ohlsson, piano	LP: Legendary Recordings LR 106 CD: Legato SRO 815
Verona April 1980	Gandolfo, piano	LP: Great Opera Performances GFC 16-17

L'abbandono

Verona April 1980	Gandolfo, piano	LP: Great Opera Performances GFC 16-17

Malinconia, ninfa gentile!

Verona April 1980	Gandolfo, piano	LP: Great Opera Performances GFC 16-17

BRUNO BETTINELLI (Born 1913)

Povera stanza mia

Rome 1957		LP: Collectors Limited Edition MDP 007 LP: Timaclub 30

GEORGES BIZET (1838-1875)

Agnus Dei

Solda Date not confirmed	Catena, organ	LP: Discocorp MLG 72
Florence March 1969	Balducci, piano	CD: Great Opera Performances GOP 717
Milan June 1970	Catena, organ	LP: Ariston CLAR 13009 LP: Oscar OSA 148

ARRIGO BOITO (1842-1918)

Mefistofele

Rio de Janeiro July 1964	Role of Margherita Orlandi-Malaspina, Labò, Siepi Teatro Municipal Orchestra & Chorus Molinari-Pradelli	Unpublished radio broadcast
Macerata July 1972	Vajna, Merighi, Siepi Macerata Opera Orchestra & Chorus Santi	LP: Historical Recording Enterprises HRE 229 Excerpts CD: Legato LCD 113
Newark NJ November 1976	Meriggioli, Campora, Hines New Jersey State Opera Orchestra and Chorus Silipigni	Unpublished radio broadcast Prison scene LP: Historical Recording Enterprises HRE 229

Mefistofele, Act 3

Amsterdam May 1973	Frusoni, Smit Netherlands RO Kersjes	LP: MRF Records MRF 152 CD: VAI Audio VAIA 1062

Mefistofele, excerpt (Spunta l'aurora pallida)

Amsterdam October 1962	Netherlands RO Vernizzi	LP: Collectors Limited Edition MDP 021 LP: Timaclub 19 CD: Great Opera Performances GOP 709 CD: Fanclub 101
Marseilles February 1973	Marseilles Opera Orchestra Bazire	CD: Bongiovanni GB 11052

Mefistofele, excerpt (L'altra notte)

Turin 1939	EIAR Orchestra Tansini	78: Cetra CC 2194/BB 25049 LP: Cetra LPC 55015/LPO 2008 LP: Ember GVC 53 CD: Cetra CDO 106 CD: Palladio PD 4162 CD: Andromeda ANR 2536/Fabbri GVS 06 CD: Great Opera Performances GOP 794 <u>CDO 106 incorrectly states that</u> <u>recording was made in 1956 and</u> <u>conducted by Simonetto</u>
Amsterdam October 1962	Netherlands RO Vernizzi	LP: Collectors Limited Edition MDP 021 LP: Discocorp MLG 72 LP: Timaclub 19 LP: Rodolphe RP 12438-12439 CD: Great Opera Performances GOP 709 CD: Fanclub 101
Florence March 1969	Balducci, piano	CD: Great Opera Performances GOP 717

BRACESCO

Ave Maria; O salutaris hostia

Solda August 1979	Montanari, organ	LP: Great Opera Performances GOP 46 CD: Great Opera Performances GOP 795

CAGGIANO

Assumpta est Maria

Solda	Montanari, organ	LP: Great Opera Performances GOP 46
August 1979		CD: Great Opera Performances GOP 795

Ave regina coelorum

Solda	Montanari, organ	LP: Great Opera Performances GOP 46
August 1981		CD: Great Opera Performances GOP 795

Il pianto della Madonna

Solda	Montanari, organ	LP: Great Opera Performances GOP 46
August 1973		CD: Great Opera Performances GOP 795

RANIERI CAPPONI (18th century)

La povera Lina

Milan	Beltrami, piano	LP: Timaclub 10
December 1971		

ALFREDO CATALANI (1854-1893)

La Wally

Bergamo	Role of Wally	LP: Morgan MOR 7201
October 1972	Zambon, Carroli	LP: Historic Operatic Treasures ERR 102
	Teatro Donizetti	CD: Foyer 2CF-2055
	Orchestra & Chorus	
	Scaglia	

La Wally, Act 4

Amsterdam	Frusoni	CD: VAI Audio VAIA 1062
May 1973	Netherlands RO	
	Kersjes	

La Wally, excerpt (Ebben? Ne andrò lontana)

Milan	RAI Milano	LP: Collectors Limited Edition MDP 007
January 1958	Orchestra	LP: Rodolphe RP 12438-12439
	Scaglia	LP: Timaclub 30
		CD: Rodolphe RPC 32656
		CD: Memories HR 4419-4420
		CD: Cetra CDMR 5024
Amsterdam	Netherlands RO	CD: Great Opera Performances GOP 728
December	Vernizzi	
1968		
Florence	Balducci, piano	CD: Great Opera Performances GOP 717
March 1969		
Marseilles	Marseilles	CD: Bongiovanni GB 11052
February	Opera Orchestra	
1973	Bazire	

Loreley, excerpt (Amor celeste ebbrezza)

Turin	RAI Torino	78: Cetra AT 0320
May 1953	Orchestra	LP: Cetra LPO 2008
	Basile	LP: OASI 540
		CD: Cetra CDO 106
		CD: Fabbri GVS 06
		CD 106 incorrectly dated 1958
Milan	RAI Milano	LP: Timaclub 30
December	Orchestra	LP: Rodolphe RP 12438-12439
1958	Mannino	CD: Rodolphe RPC 32656
		CD: Melodram MEL 27025
		CD: Cetra CDMR 5020

GUSTAVE CHARPENTIER (1860-1950)

Louise, excerpt (Depuis le jour)

Turin December 1949	RAI Torino Orchestra Simonetto Sung in Italian	78: Cetra BB 25272 LP: Cetra LPC 55015/LPO 2041 LP: Ember GVC 53 LP: Collectors Limited edition MDP 007 CD: Palladio PD 4162 CD: Great Opera Performances GOP 794 CD: Fabbri GVS 06
Trieste October 1975	Silvestri, piano	CD: Eklipse EKR 6

LUIGI CHERUBINI (1760-1842)

Medea

Dallas November 1967	Role of Medea Casoni, Sciutti, Prevedi, Zaccaria Dallas Civic Opera Orchestra & Chorus Rescigno	LP: MRF Records MRF 3 LP: CLS Records AMDRL 32817 LP: Historical Recording Enterprises HRE 258 CD: Music and Arts CD 670 CD: Great Opera Performances GOP 755 GOP 755 also includes piano rehearsal extracts Excerpts LP: Discocorp MLG 72
Amsterdam June 1970	Gilles, Spek, Picchi, Smit Netherlands Radio Orchestra & Chorus Vernizzi	Unpublished radio broadcast
Montova January 1971	Baggiore, Foglizzo, Loferese, Gambelli Teatro Social Orchestra & Chorus Rescigno	CD: Myto MCD 91136

FREDERIC CHOPIN (1810-1849)

Maiden's wish

Voghera October 1981	Gandolfo, piano Sung in Italian	LP: Great Opera Performances GFC 16-17 CD: Great Opera Performances GOP 795

FRANCESCO CILEA (1866-1950)

Adriana Lecouvreur

Naples November 1959	Role of Adriana Simionato, Corelli, Bastianini San Carlo Orchestra & Chorus Rossi	LP: Ed Smith UORC 497 LP: Hope Records HOPE 246 LP: MRF Records MRF 47 LP: Morgan MOR 5901 LP: Melodram MEL 043 LP: Discocorp IGI 294 LP: Replica RPL 2454-2456 LP: Cetra DOC 19 CD: Melodram MEL 27009 CD: Phoenix PX 5022 Excerpts LP: Rodolphe RP 12438-12439 CD: Rodolphe RPC 32656 CD: Memories HR 4400-4401
Edinburgh August 1963	Lazzarini, Oncina, Bruscantini San Carlo Orchestra & Chorus De Fabritiis	Unpublished radio broadcast Excerpts LP: Discocorp MLG 72
Rio de Janeiro August 1964	Lazzarini, Loforese, Fortes Teatro Colon Orchestra & Chorus Molinari-Pradelli	Unpublished radio broadcast
Amsterdam November 1965	Aarden, Ferrari, Capecchi Netherlands Radio Orchestra & Chorus Vernizzi	CD: Verona 27077-27078
Milan November 1965	Rota, Oncina, Campi RAI Milano Orchestra & Chorus De Fabritiis	Unpublished radio broadcast
Hartford Connecticut October 1969	Dunn, Lavirgen, Medones Orchestra & Chorus Moresco	Unpublished radio broadcast

Adriana Lecouvreur/concluded

Caracas May 1972	Cipriani, Domingo, Sardinero Venezuela SO and Chorus Veltri	Unpublished radio broadcast
Newark NJ November 1973	Nave, Domingo, Sordello New Jersey State Opera Orchestra and Chorus Silipigni	LP: PCL 1001-1003 CD: Legato LCD 140
Genova April 1982	Lazzarini, Garaventa, Basiola Teatro Communale Orchestra & Chorus Previtali	Unpublished radio broadcast

Adriana Lecouvreur, abridged version with piano

Milan April 1993	Moretto, Cupido, Mori Gandolfo, piano	CD: Bongiovanni GB 25152 <u>Fragments also on VHS Video published</u> <u>by Bel Canto Society BCS 0115</u>

Adriana Lecouvreur, Act 4

Amsterdam May 1973	Frusoni, Smit Netherlands RO Kersjes	CD: VAI Audio VAIA 1062

Adriana Lecouvreur, excerpt (La dolcissima effige)

Rome March 1940	Gigli Rome Opera Orchestra De Fabritiis	LP: Timaclub 30 LP: Collectors Limited Edition MDP 018 LP: EMI 3C 153 54010-54017M LP: Rodolphe RP 12438-12439 CD: Rodolphe RPC 32656 CD: Eklipse EKR 30

Adriana Lecouvreur, excerpt (Io son l'umile ancella)

Turin June 1940	EIAR Orchestra Tansini	78: Cetra BB 25028/CB 20149 45: Cetra SPO 1015 LP: Cetra LPC 55015/LPO 2008/SKI 7011 LP: Ember GVC 53 CD: Cetra CDO 106 CD: Palladio PD 4162 CD: Andromeda ANR 2536/Fabbri GVS 06 CD: Great Opera Performances GOP 794 <u>CDO 106 incorrectly dated 1954</u>
Amsterdam October 1962	Netherlands RO Vernizzi	LP: Collectors Limited Edition MDP 021 LP: Timaclub 19/Timaclub 21 CD: Great Opera Performances GOP 709 CD: Fanclub 101
Dallas November 1968	Dallas Civic Opera Orchestra Rescigno	LP: Historical Recording Enterprises HRE 280 CD: Music and Arts CD 670
Florence March 1969	Balducci, piano	CD: Great Opera Performances GOP 717
Padua April 1971	Corradetti, piano	CD: Myto MCD 93383
Marseilles February 1973	Marseilles Opera Orchestra Bazire	CD: Bongiovanni GB 11052
Pistoia March 1973	Gandolfo, piano	CD: Great Opera Performances GOP 795
New York October 1979	Ohlsson, piano	LP: Legendary Recordings LR 106
Verona April 1980	Gandolfo, piano	LP: Great Opera Performances GFC 16-17

20/6 Amsterdam   **1970**
Concertgebouw 15.00 uur
(concertuitvoering)

MEDEA

Luigi Cherubini
Tekst François Benoit Hoffman
Dirigent Fulvio Vernizzi
Het Omroeporkest
Het Groot Omroepkoor

Magda Olivero	*Medea*
Marie Louise Gilles	*Neris*
Nelly van der Spek	*Glauce*
Mirto Picchi	*Giasone*
Henk Smit	*Creonte*
Geraldine Hacket-Jones	*1e dienstmaagd*
Sylvia Suri	*2e dienstmaagd*
Piet van Meulen	*Hoofd van de wacht*

pauze na het eerste bedrijf

EVEREST/SCALA

GREAT VOICES OF THE CENTURY

MAGDA OLIVERO

Great Scenes from Puccini's
TURANDOT

SIDE A
Popolo di Pekino! (Act I)
Notte senza un lumicino; Signore, ascolta! (finale, Act I)

SIDE B
Nella cupa notte (the riddle) (Act II)
Il nome che cercate; Principessa, l'amore (Death of Liu, Act III)

SC-880

Adriana Lecouvreur, excerpt (Poveri fiori)

Turin November 1939	EIAR Orchestra Tansini	78: Cetra BB 25028/BB 25049/ CB 20149/CC 2194 45: Cetra SPO 1015 LP: Cetra LPC 55015/LPC 55050/LPO 2008 LP: Ember GVC 53 CD: Cetra CDO 106 CD: Palladio PD 4162 CD: Andromeda ANR 2536 CD: Fabbri GVS 06 CD: Great Opera Performances GOP 794 Some early issues name conductor as La Rosa Parodi; CDO 106 incorrectly dated 1964
Florence March 1969	Balducci, piano	CD: Great Opera Performances GOP 717
Dallas November 1970	Dallas Civic Opera Orchestra Rescigno	LP: Historical Recording Enterprises CD: Music and Arts CD 670
Padua April 1971	Corradetti, piano	CD: Myto MCD 93383
Marseilles February 1973	Marseilles Opera Orchestra Bazire	CD: Bongiovanni GB 11052
New York October 1979	Ohlsson, piano	LP: Legendary Recordings LR 106
Verona April 1980	Gandolfo, piano	LP: Great Opera Performances GFC 16-17
Voghera October 1981	Gandolfo, piano	CD: Great Opera Performances GOP 795

CLAUDE DEBUSSY (1862-1918)

L'enfant prodigue, excerpt (Air de Lia)

New York October 1979	Ohlsson, piano	LP: Legendary Recordings LR 106
Verona April 1980	Gandolfo, piano	LP: Great Opera Performances GFC 16-17

LUIGI DENZA (1846-1922)

Si vous l'aviez compris

Rome February 1973	Cafaro, piano	LP: Timaclub 10
Pistoia March 1973	Gandolfo, piano	CD: Great Opera Performances GOP 795

STEFANO DONAUDY (1879-1925)

O del mio amato ben

New York December 1977	Davis, piano	LP: Legendary Recordings LR 106
Dallas December 1977	Davis, piano	CD: Legato SRO 815
Voghera October 1981	Gandolfo, piano	LP: Great Opera Performances GFC 16-17 CD: Great Opera Performances GOP 795

Sorga il cor

Dallas December 1977	Davis, piano	CD: Legato SRO 815

Spirate pur

Dallas December 1977	Davis, piano	CD: Legato SRO 815

Vaghissima sembranza

New York December 1977	Davis, piano	LP: Legendary Recordings LR 106
Dallas December 1977	Davis, piano	CD: Legato SRO 815
Voghera October 1981	Gandolfo, piano	LP: Great Opera Performances GFC 16-17 CD: Great Opera Performances GOP 795

HENRI DUPARC (1848-1933)

Chanson triste

Voghera October 1981	Gandolfo, piano	LP: Great Opera Performances GFC 16-17 CD: Great Opera Performances GOP 795

GOTTFRIED VON EINEM (1918-1996)

Der Besuch der alten Dame

Naples February 1977	<u>Role of Claire</u> Ferraro, Cesari, Vernetti San Carlo Orchestra & Chorus Gracis <u>Sung in Italian</u>	Unpublished radio broadcast

SAMMY FAIN (1902-1989)

Love is a many splendoured thing

Rome December 1957 or February 1964	Unidentified accompaniment <u>Sung in Italian</u>	LP: Discocorp MLG 72

GABRIEL FAURE (1845-1924)

Après un rêve

Verona April 1980	Gandolfo, piano	LP: Great Opera Performances GFC 16-17
Voghera October 1981	Gandolfo, piano	CD: Great Opera Performances GOP 795

CESAR FRANCK (1822-1890)

Panis angelicus

Milan June 1970	Catena, organ	LP: Ariston CLAR 13009 LP: Oscar OS 148
Trieste October 1975	Silvestri, piano	CD: Eklipse EKR 6

La procession

Turin May 1953	Magnetti, piano	78: Cetra PE 184 LP: Cetra LPC 55011 CD: Fabbri GVS 06

SANDRO FUGA (Born 1906)

Confesssione

Turin May 1971	Ghitti, Basiola Teatro Regio Orchestra Rivoli	Unpublished radio broadcast

Puccini

MANON LESCAUT

Magda Olivero
Manon Lescaut

Richard Tucker
Des Grieux

Vincente Sardinero   Lescaut
Eugene Green   Geronte
Bernard Fitch   Edmondo

Michelangelo Veltri
Conductor

Caracas

June 2, 1972

LEGATO CLASSICS

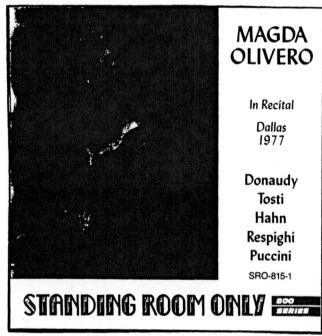

MAGDA OLIVERO

In Recital

Dallas
1977

**Donaudy
Tosti
Hahn
Respighi
Puccini**

SRO-815-1

STANDING ROOM ONLY 800 SERIES

GRANDI VOCI
ALLA SCALA

Magda
Olivero

CON IL PATROCINIO DEL
TEATRO ALLA SCALA

FABBRI EDITORI

Mascagni · Iris
Magda Olivero · Salvatore Puma
Saturno Meletti
Orchestra Sinfonica e Coro di Torino della Rai
Angelo Questa

CETRA

Emozioni

Digitally
Remastered

GALLETTI

Ab ortu solis

Solda	Montanari, organ	LP: Great Opera Performances GOP 46
1987		CD: Great Opera Performances GOP 795

OTTORINO GENTILUCCI

Don Ciccio

Milan	Amadini, Cioni,	Unpublished radio broadcast
April 1958	Novelli	
	RAI Milano	
	Orchestra	
	Gatto	

GERUSSI

Panteismo

Turin	Megnetti, piano	78: Cetra AT 0322
May 1953		LP: OASI 540
		CD: Fabbri GVS 06
		This recording also used as soundtrack
		for a TV performance now published on
		VHS Video by Bel Canto Society BCS 0115

UMBERTO GIORDANO (1867-1948)

Fedora

Brescia February 1968	Role of Fedora Antonioli, Pedrini Teatro Grande Orchestra & Chorus F.Patané	Unpublished radio broadcast
Monte Carlo May 1969	Del Monaco, Gobbi Monte Carlo Opera Orchestra & Chorus Gardelli	LP: Decca SET 435-436 CD: Decca 433 0332
Lucca September 1969	Di Stefano, Mazzini Teatro Communale Orchestra & Chorus Annovazzi	LP: Estro armonico EA 047 CD: Di Stefano GDS 109 CD: Great Opera Performances GOP 717
Dallas November 1969	Prevedi, Zaccaria Dallas Civic Opera Orchestra and Chorus Rescigno	CD: Music and Arts CD 671
Trenton NJ November 1971	Campora, Bardelli New Jersey State Opera Orchestra and Chorus Silipigni	Unpublished radio broadcast

Fedora, extracts

Piacenza January 1972	Giacomini ATER Orchestra Braggio	LP: Bongiovanni GAO 189-190

Fedora, Act 3

Amsterdam May 1967	Antonioli, Protti Netherlands Radio Orchestra & Chorus Vernizzi	LP: Historical Recording Enterprises HRE 218 CD: Verona 28016-28017 CD: Great Opera Performances GOP 709

Andrea Chenier, excerpt (La mamma morta)

Milan	RAI Milano	LP: Collectors Limited Edition MDP 007
January	Orchestra	LP: Timaclub 30
1958	Scaglia	LP: Rodolphe RP 12438-12439
		CD: Rodolphe RPC 32656

Amsterdam	Netherlands RO	CD: Great Opera Performances GOP 728
October	Vernizzi	
1968		

CHARLES GOUNOD (1818-1893)

Adoro te devote

Milan	Catena, organ	LP: Ariston CLAR 13009
June 1970		LP: Oscar OSA 148

Ave Maria

Florence	Balducci, piano	CD: Great Opera Performances GOP 717
March 1969		

Milan	Catena, organ	LP: Ariston CLAR 13009
June 1970		LP: Oscar OSA 148

ALEXANDER GRETCHANINOV (1864-1956)

Over the steppe

Turin	Megnetti, piano	78: Cetra AT 0322
May 1953	Sung in Italian	LP: OASI 540
		CD: Fabbri GVS 06

GUERCIA

Non m'amava

Rome	Cafaro, piano	LP: Timaclub 10
February		
1973		

Pistoia	Gandolfo, piano	CD: Great Opera Performances GOP 795
March 1973		

REYNALDO HAHN (1875-1947)

D'une prison

Dallas December 1977	Davis, piano	CD: Legato SRO 815
Verona April 1980	Gandolfo, piano	LP: Great Opera Performances GFC 16-17
Voghera October 1981	Gandolfo, piano	CD: Great Opera Performances GOP 795

L'heure exquise

Dallas December 1977	Davis, piano	CD: Legato SRO 815

Le plus beau présent

Dallas December 1977	Davis, piano	CD: Legato SRO 815

Si mes vers avaient des ailes

Dallas December 1977	Davis, piano	CD: Legato SRO 815
Verona April 1980	Gandolfo, piano	LP: Great Opera Performances GFC 16-17
Voghera October 1981	Gandolfo, piano	CD: Great Opera Performances GOP 795

LES LUNDIS MUSICAUX
DE L'ATHÉNÉE
SAISON 1979-1980

**10 DÉCEMBRE
1979 / RÉF. B**

MAGDA OLIVERO SOPRANO
MARYLENE DOSSE PIANO

**BELLINI/MASSENET/DEBUSSY/PUCCINI/
LEONCAVALLO**

PROGRAMME

Magda Olivero et Marylène Dosse

Vincenzo Bellini	"Malinconia, ninfa gentile"
	"L'Abbandono"
	"Oh ! quante volte, oh ! quante"
	(de "I Capuletti e I Montecchi")

Marylène Dosse

Alexandre Scriabine	Trois Etudes
	Opus 8, n° 11
	Opus 8, n° 2
	Opus 8, n° 12

Magda Olivero et Marylène Dosse :

Gioacchino Rossini	"L'Invito"
Ruggero Leoncavallo	"Mattinatta"
Ottorino Respighi	"Nebbie"

Entracte

Magda Olivero et Marylène Dosse

Gabriel Fauré	"Après un rêve"
Reynaldo Hahn	"D'une prison"
	"Si mes vers avaient des ailes"

Marylène Dosse

Enrique Granados	Valses Poétiques

Magda Olivero et Marylène Dosse

Jules Massenet	"Elegie"
	"Adieu, notre petite table"
	(de "Manon")
Claude Debussy	"Air de Lia"
	(de "L'Enfant Prodigue")
Francesco Cilea	"Poveri fiori"
	"Io son l'umile ancella"
	(de "Adrienne Lecouvreur")

GEORGE FRIDERIC HANDEL (1685-1759)

Serse, excerpt (Ombra mai fù)

Milan January 1958	RAI Milano Orchestra Scaglia	LP: Collectors Limited Edition MDP 007 LP: Timaclub 21/Timaclub 30 LP: Rodolphe RP 12438-12439 CD: Rodolphe RPC 32656 CD: Melodram MEL 27025 Rodolphe incorrectly names conductor as Mannino
Milan June 1970	Catena, organ	LP: Ariston CLAR 13009 LP: Oscar OSA 148

LEOS JANACEK (1854-1928)

Jenufa

Milan April 1974	Role of Kostelnicka Bumbry, Baglioni, Cioni, Merolla, Zaccaria La Scala Orchestra and Chorus Semkow Sung in Italian	LP: Morgan MOR 7401 CD: Myto MCD 961142

DE LIGUORI

Tu scendi dalle stelle

Vatican City December 1959	Unnamed accompanist	LP: Timaclub 21
Solda 1987	Montanari, organ	LP: Great Opera Performances GOP 46 CD: Great Opera Performances GOP 795

RUGGERO LEONCAVALLO (1858-1919)

Ave Maria

Solda 1987	Montanari, organ	LP: Great Opera Performances GOP 46 CD: Great Opera Performances GOP 795

Mattinata

New York October 1979	Ohlsson, piano	LP: Legendary Recordings LR 106
Verona April 1980	Gandolfo, piano	LP: Great Opera Performances GFC 16-17
Voghera October 1981	Gandolfo, piano	CD: Great Opera Performances GOP 795

LUZZI

Ave Maria

Solda August 1981	Montanari, organ	LP: Great Opera Performances GOP 46 CD: Great Opera Performances GOP 795

GIAN FRANCESCO MALIPIERO (1882-1973)

Orfeide

Florence June 1966	Misciano, Capecchi Maggio musicale Orchestra & Chorus Scherchen	CD: Tahra TAH 190-191

PIETRO MASCAGNI (1863-1945)

L'amico Fritz, excerpt (Son pochi fiori)

Amsterdam	Netherlands RO	LP: Collectors Limited Edition MDP 021
December 1968	Vernizzi	CD: Great Opera Performances GOP 728

L'amico Fritz, excerpt (Non mi resta che il pianto)

Amsterdam	Netherlands RO	LP: Collectors Limited Edition MDP 021
December 1968	Vernizzi	CD: Great Opera Performances GOP 728

L'amico Fritz, excerpt (Suzel, buon dí!)

Turin	Tagliavini	78: Cetra BB 25050/CC 2224
November	EIAR Orchestra	45: Cetra SPO 1076/CS 7
1939	Tansini	LP: OASI 540
		CD: Centaur CRC 2164
		CD: Great Opera Performances GOP 794
		Conductor of this recording was sometimes mistakenly thought to be Mascagni
Milan	Villi	LP: Collectors Limited Edition MDP 007
1958	Unspecified orchestra and conductor	LP: Timaclub MPV 24-25
		Recording incomplete

Cavalleria rusticana, excerpts (Voi lo sapete; Regina coeli)

Amsterdam	Netherlands Radio	LP: Collectors Limited Edition MDP 021
December 1968	Orchestra & Chorus Vernizzi	CD: Great Opera Performances GOP 728

Cavalleria rusticana, Intermezzo arrangement

Solda	Montanari, organ	LP: Great Opera Performances GOP 46
1994		CD: Great Opera Performances GOP 795

Iris

Turin September 1956	Role of Iris Puma, Neri RAI Torino Orchestra & Chorus Questa	LP: MRF Records MRF 29 LP: Estro armonico EA 030 LP: Cetra LAR 23 CD: Cetra CDAR 2023 Excerpts LP: Rococo 1016 Estro armonico incorrectly dated February 1962
Amsterdam October 1963	Ottolini, Capecchi Netherlands Radio Orchestra & Chorus Vernizzi	LP: MRF Records MRF 151 CD: Verona 27014-27015 CD: Great Opera Performances GOP 708 Excerpts CD: Fanclub 101

Iris, scenes from Acts 2 and 3

Amsterdam June 1966	Gismondo, Basiola Netherlands RO De Fabritiis	CD: VAI Audio VAIA 1062

Iris, excerpt (Un dì ero piccino)

Turin May 1953	RAI Torino Orchestra Basile	78: Cetra AT 0321 LP: Cetra LPC 55011 CD: Cetra CDO 106 CD: Palladio PD 4162 CD: Fabbri GVS 06 This recording also used as soundtrack for a TV performance now published on VHS Video by Bel Canto Society BCS 0115
Amsterdam October 1962	Netherlands RO Vernizzi	LP: Collectors Limited Edition MDP 021 CD: Great Opera Performances GOP 709 CD: Fanclub 101
Trieste October 1975	Silvestri, piano	CD: Eklipse EKR 6

Lodoletta, excerpt (Flammen perdonami!)

Voghera October 1981	Gandolfo, piano	LP: Great Opera Performances GFC 16-17 CD: Great Opera Performances GOP 795

JULES MASSENET (1842–1912)

Werther

Turin	Role of Charlotte	LP: Discocorp RR 513
June 1963	Panni, Lazzari,	CD: Melodram CDM 27065
	Badioli	Excerpts
	RAI Torino	LP: PCL 1001–1003
	Orchestra & Chorus	LP: Timaclub 2G2KP 19083–19084
	Rossi	
	Sung in Italian	

Manon, extracts (Je suis encore toute étourdie; Restons ici!; Adieu, notre petite table; Toi! Vous!)

Turin	Vendittelli	LP: MRF Records MRF 129
July 1975	RAI Torino	LP: Timaclub 30
	Orchestra	CD: Bella voce BLV 107 221
	Argento	

Manon, excerpt (Restons ici!/Voyons Manon!)

Milan	RAI Milano	LP: Collectors Limited Edition MDP 007
January	Orchestra	LP: Rodolphe RP 12438–12439
1958	Scaglia	
	Sung in Italian	

Elégie

Verona	Gandolfo, piano	LP: Great Opera Performances
April 1980		GFC 16–17

Manon, excerpt (Adieu, notre petite table)

Turin May 1953	RAI Torino Orchestra Basile Sung in Italian	78: Cetra PE 184 LP: Cetra LPC 55011/LPO 2041 CD: Palladio PD 4162 CD: Fabbri GVS 06
Florence March 1969	Balducci, piano Sung in Italian	CD: Great Opera Performances GOP 717
Padua April 1971	Corradetti, piano Sung in Italian	CD: Myto MCD 93383
Trieste October 1975	Silvestri, piano	CD: Eklipse EKR 6
New York October 1979	Ohlsson, piano	LP: Legendary Recordings LR 106
Verona April 1980	Gandolfo, piano	LP: Great Opera Performances GFC 16-17
Vienna October 1981	Schneider, piano	CD: Legato SRO 815
Voghera October 1981	Gandolfo, piano	CD: Great Opera Performances GOP 795

TITO MATTEI (1841-1914)

Reste avec moi!

Rome February 1973	Cafaro, piano	LP: Timaclub 10
Pistoia March 1973	Gandolfo, piano	CD: Great Opera Performances GOP 795

GIUSEPPE MERCADANTE (1795–1870)

Le 7 parole di Nostro Signore, excerpt (Di mille colpe reo)

Details not confirmed	Unnamed accompaniment	LP: MRF Records MRF 88

Pelagio, excerpt (Aria di Bianca)

Padua April 1971	Corradetti, piano	CD: Myto MCD 93383
Amsterdam March 1972	Netherlands RO Kersjes	LP: Timaclub 19 LP: MRF Records MRF 88

Salve Maria

Milan June 1970	Catena, organ	LP: Ariston CLAR 13009 LP: Oscar OSA 148

MILILOTTI

Ad una stella

Rome 1957	Unnamed accompaniment	LP: Collectors Limited Edition MDP 007 LP: Timaclub 30

WOLFGANG AMADEUS MOZART (1756–1791)

Agnus Dei (Mass in C minor), arrangement
Incorrectly described as Ave verum corpus

Milan June 1970	Catena, organ	LP: Ariston CLAR 13009 LP: Oscar OSA 148
Solda August 1981	Montanari, organ	LP: Great Opera Performances GOP 46 CD: Great Opera Performances GOP 795

ERRICO PETRELLA (1813-1877)

I promessi sposi

San Remo December 1973	Campora, Salvadori San Remo SO and Chorus Farina	CD: Great Opera Performances GOP 744 Excerpts LP: Voce 53 LP: Timaclub 12

RICCARDO PICK-MANGIAGALLI (1882-1949)

Il carillon magico

Amsterdam October 1962	Netherlands RO Vernizzi	CD: Great Opera Performances GOP 709

CICO PINSUTTI (1829-1888)

Il libro santo

Milan December 1971	Beltrami, piano	LP: Timaclub 10

AMILCARE PONCHIELLI (1834-1886)

I promessi sposi

San Remo December 1973	Campora, Salvadori San Remo SO and Chorus Farina	CD: Great Opera Performances GOP 744 Excerpts LP: Voce 53 LP: Timaclub 12

The operas by Petrella and Ponchielli were given in abbreviated concert form
in a double bill

NINO PORTO

Liriche da camera, song cycle

Turin	G.Gatti	LP: Timaclub 33
December	Cassardo, piano	CD: Bongiovanni
1974	Conti, piano	The poems of this cycle are also recited
		by the various poets

FRANCIS POULENC (1899-1963)

La voix humaine

Venice	La Fenice	LP: Morgan MOR 7004
May 1970	Orchestra	
	Rescigno	
Dallas	Dallas Civic	LP: Historical Recording Enterprises
November	Opera Orchestra	HRE 280
1970	Rescigno	CD: Music and Arts CD 671
San Francisco	San Francisco SO	Unpublished radio broadcast
October	Giovaninetti	
1979		

ETTORE POZZOLI (1873-1957)

Anima Christi

Solda	Montanari, organ	LP: Great Opera Performances GOP 46
August 1987		CD: Great Opera Performances GOP 795

GIACOMO PUCCINI (1858–1924)

La Bohème

Zagabria May 1964	Role of Mimì Otta, Oncina, Lovric Zagabria Opera Orchestra & Chorus Hubada	Unpublished radio broadcast Excerpts CD: Melodram MEL 27025

La Bohème, excerpt (Entrance of Mimì....to end of Act 1)

Amsterdam March 1968	Lega, Niessen Netherlands RO Vernizzi	LP: Morgan MOR 003 LP: Discocorp IGI 303 LP: Collectors Limited Edition MDP 011 CD: Verona 28016-28017 CD: Great Opera Performances GOP 728 Excerpt LP: Discocorp MLG 72 Morgan incorrectly dated May 1968

La Bohème, excerpt (Entrance of Mimì....to end of Act 3)

Amsterdam March 1968	Ostar, Lega, Niessen Netherlands RO Vernizzi	LP: Morgan MOR 003 LP: Discocorp IGI 303/AA 100 LP: Collectors Limited Edition MDP 011 LP: Historical Recording Enterprises HRE 218 CD: Verona 28016-28017 CD: Great Opera Performances GOP 728 Excerpts LP: Discocorp MLG 72 CD: Fanclub 101 Morgan incorrectly dated May 1968; HRE incorrectly states tenor to be Buzea

La Bohème, excerpt (Sono andati....to end of Act 4)

Amsterdam March 1968	Ostar, Lega, Niessen Netherlands RO Vernizzi	LP: Morgan MOR 003 LP: Discocorp IGI 303/AA 100 LP: Collectors Limited Edition MDP 011 LP: Historical Recording Enterprises HRE 218 CD: Verona 28016-28017 CD: Great Opera Performances GOP 728 Excerpt CD: Fanclub 101 Morgan incorrectly dated May 1968; HRE incorrectly states tenor to be Buzea

La Bohème, excerpt (Sì mi chiamano Mimì)

Turin 1940	EIAR Orchestra Tansini	78: Cetra BB 25053/CC 2227 LP: Cetra LPC 55015/LPO 2041 LP: Ember GVC 53 CD: Cetra CDO 106 CD: Palladio PD 4162 CD: Andromeda ANR 2536 CD: Great Opera Performances GOP 794 <u>CDO 106 incorrectly dated 1956</u>
Florence March 1969	Balducci, piano	CD: Great Opera Performances GOP 717
New York October 1979	Ohlsson, piano	LP: Legendary Recordings LR 106

La Bohème, excerpt (Donde lieta uscì)

Turin December 1949	RAI Torino Orchestra Simonetto	78: Cetra BB 25272 LP: Cetra LPC 55011/LPO 2008 CD: Cetra CDO 106 CD: Palladio PD 4162 CD: Andromeda ANR 2536 CD: Fabbri GVS 06 <u>CDO 106 incorrectly dated 1956</u>
Rome May 1958	RAI Roma Orchestra	LP: Collectors Limited Edition MDP 007 <u>Recording incomplete</u>
Dallas November 1968	Dallas Civic Opera Orchestra Rescigno	LP: Historical Recording Enterprises HRE 280 CD: Music and Arts CD 670

La Bohème, excerpt (O soave fanciulla)

Marseilles February 1973	Labò Marseilles Opera Orchestra Bazire	CD: Bongiovanni GB 11052

La Bohème, excerpt (Quando m'en vo)

Dallas November 1968	Dallas Civic Opera Orchestra Rescigno	LP: Historical Recording Enterprises HRE 280 CD: Music and Arts CD 670

La fanciulla del West

Rome March 1957	Role of Minnie Lauri-Volpi, Guelfi Rome Opera Orchestra & Chorus Bellezza	LP: Ed Smith EJS 552
Rio de Janeiro July 1964	Gibin, Guelfi Teatro Municipal Orchestra & Chorus Molinari-Pradelli	Unpublished radio broadcast
Trieste March 1965	Limarilli, Puglisi Teatro Verdi Orchestra & Chorus Basile	LP: Morgan MOR 6501 CD: Nuova Era NE 2324-2325
Turin May 1966	Limarilli, Colzani Teatro Regio Orchestra & Chorus Previtali	LP: MRF Records MRF 112 Excerpt LP: Opus 82
Venice February 1967	Barioni, Guelfi La Fenice Orchestra & Chorus Fabritiis	CD: Myto MCD 93383

La fanciulla del West, excerpt (Laggiù nel Soledad)

Hilversum December 1968	Netherlands RO Vernizzi	CD: Great Opera Performances GOP 728
Amsterdam March 1972	Netherlands RO Kersjes	LP: Timaclub 19 CD: Fanclub 101

Gianni Schicchi, excerpt (O mio babbino caro)

Turin May 1953	RAI Torino Orchestra Basile	78: Cetra AT 0321 LP: Cetra LPC 55011/LPO 2041 CD: Palladio PD 4162
Hilversum December 1968	Netherlands RO Vernizzi	CD: Great Opera Performances GOP 728 CD: Fanclub 101

Madama Butterfly

Naples December 1961	Role of Butterfly Borelli, Cioni, Zanasi San Carlo Orchestra & Chorus Rescigno	LP: Historical Recording Enterprises HRE 273 CD: Great Opera Performances GOP 731

Madama Butterfly, excerpts (Ancora un passo; Che tua madre; Con onor muore)

Amsterdam December 1968	Netherlands Radio Orchestra & Chorus Vernizzi	CD: Great Opera Performances GOP 728

Madama Butterfly, excerpt (Vieni la sera)

Amsterdam March 1968	Lega Netherlands RO Vernizzi	LP: Timaclub 19 LP: Discocorp IGI 303 LP: Rodolphe RP 12438-12439 CD: Great Opera Performances GOP 728

Madama Butterfly, excerpt (Un bel dl)

Amsterdam December 1968	Netherlands RO Vernizzi	CD: Fanclub 101
Florence March 1969	Balducci, piano	CD: Great Opera Performances GOP 717

Madama Butterfly, excerpt (Legger con me volete questa lettera?)

Ferrara September 1974	D'Orazi Gandolfo, piano	CD: Great Opera Performances GOP 731

Manon Lescaut

Amsterdam October 1964	Role of Manon Borsò, Lidonni, Foiani Concertgebouw Orchestra & Chorus Vernizzi	LP: Great Operatic Performances GFC 19-20 CD: Bella Voce BLV 107221 CD: Eklipse EKR 6 Excerpts LP: BJR Records BJR 119 LP: OASI 540 CD: Fanclub 101
Verona July 1970	Domingo, Fioravanti, Mariotti Arena di Verona Orchestra & Chorus Santi	CD: Foyer 2CF-2033 Excerpts CD: Myto MCD 90421
Lucca September 1970	Cioni, Mazzini, Clabassi Teatro Communale Orchestra & Chorus Verchi	Unpublished radio broadcast
Genova March 1971	Ilosfalvy, Cocchieri, Campi Teatro Communale Orchestra & Chorus G.Patané	Unpublished radio broadcast
Caracas June 1972	Tucker, Sardinero, Green Venezuela SO and Chorus Veltri	LP: Historic Operatic Treasures ERR 130 LP: Historical Recording Enterprises HRE 354 CD: Legato LCD 113

Manon Lescaut, excerpt (Tu, tu, amore!)

Marseilles February 1973	Labò Marseilles Opera Orchestra Bazire	CD: Bongiovanni GB 11052
Turin July 1975	Venditelli RAI Torino Orchestra Argento	CD: Bella voce BLV 107 221

MASTERCLASSES

Magda Olivero & Tom Krause
Italiaanse opera   *orkestliederen*

30/31 augustus, 1 september 1993
10-15 uur, 16-18 uur, 20-22 uur
2 september 13-18 uur, 3 september 10-15 uur
dagkaarten ƒ 10,- alleen aan de zaal, geen telefonische reserveringen

40 jaar Internationaal Vocalisten Concours
Casinotheater aan de Parade 's-Hertogenbosch

Carnegie Hall

1977-1978 SEASON

Monday Evening, December 5, 1977 at 8:00

MATTHEWS/NAPAL LTD. presents

MAGDA OLIVERO
Soprano

IVAN DAVIS
Piano

In Joint Concert

There is a long and honored tradition for a collaboration between a great singer and a virtuoso pianist. Consider some of the remarkable such pairings in the last 150 years: Viardot and Chopin, Garden and Gieseking, Teyte and Cortot, Koshetz and Rachmaninov, and more recently de los Angeles and de Larrocha, Fischer-Dieskau and Horowitz, Pears and Perahia.

In such circumstances a recital becomes something more; it is vocal chamber music, a partnership of equals. Magda Olivero joins Ivan Davis in not only a bond of music, but one of friendship to explore song in many guises, to recreate an evening which might have been heard in a drawing room in the early decades of this century.

Program notes by John Ardoin

I

Stefano Donaudy was born of a French father and an Italian mother in Palermo in 1879. He died in Naples in 1925. Though he wrote a half-dozen operas and a symphonic poem, he is remembered today for his 36 "Arie di stile antico," or "songs in an old style," which have been favorites with singers from Caruso and McCormack to Muzio and Albanese.

Spirate pur, spirate...

Inspire, then...
Encircle my love gentle breezes
And reassure yourself that she keeps me
  in her heart.

Vaghissima sembianza

Most charming look of an ancient, beloved
  woman,
Who has been painted with so fine a likeness,
That I look and I speak and I believe

As if she before me were as real as a beauti-
  ful day of love.
The dearest memory which is awakened in
  my heart so ardently,
Has caused hope to be born,
That a kiss, a wish, a cry of love
No longer cries out to one who is silent
  forever.

Sorgi il sol!

The sun is up,
What are you doing?
If you are asleep—wake up!
It's spring.
If you are awake—get up!
Come to joy.
The time has come to hasten again to the
  fields sparkling with a thousand colors,
To set a song free,
To gather flowers,
To shout along the shore,
To fill one's heart with the joy of love.
If you don't come, the flowers won't bloom.

Exclusive Management
MATTHEWS/NAPAL LTD.
270 West End Avenue
New York, N.Y. 10023

Baldwin Piano   London Records

Manon Lescaut, excerpt (In quelle trine morbide)

Turin December 1949	EIAR Orchestra Simonetto	78: Cetra BB 25271 LP: Cetra LPC 55011/LPC 55050/ LPO 2041/SKI 7009 CD: Cetra CDO 106 CD: Palladio PD 4162 CD: Andromeda ANR 2536/Fabbri GVS 06 <u>CDO 106 incorrectly dated 1958</u>
Milan January 1958	RAI Milano Orchestra Scaglia	LP: Collectors Limited Edition MDP 007 LP: Timaclub 30 LP: Rodolphe RP 12438-12439 CD: Cetra CDMR 5024 CD: Memories HR 4419-4420
Amsterdam October 1962	Netherlands RO Vernizzi	CD: Great Opera Performances GOP 709
Padua April 1971	Corradetti, piano	CD: Myto MCD 93383
Marseilles February 1973	Marseilles Opera Orchestra Bazire	CD: Bongiovanni GB 11052 CD: Fanclub 101
Pistoia March 1973	Gandolfo, piano	CD: Great Opera Performances GOP 795

Manon Lescaut, excerpt (Sola perduta abbandonata)

Turin November 1950	RAI Torino Orchestra Simonetto	78: Cetra BB 25277 LP: Cetra LPC 55011/LPO 2008 CD: Cetra CDO 106 CD: Palladio PD 4162 CD: Andromeda ANR 2536/Fabbri GVS 06 <u>CDO 106 incorrectly dated 1958</u>
Florence March 1969	Balducci, piano	CD: Great Opera Performances GOP 717
Pistoia March 1973	Gandolfo, piano	CD: Great Opera Performances GOP 795
Trieste October 1975	Silvestri, piano	CD: Eklipse EKR 6 CD: Myto MCD 93383
Dallas December 1977	Davis, piano	CD: Legato SRO 815
New York October 1979	Ohlsson, piano	LP: Legendary Recordings LR 106

Manon Lescaut/Sola perduta abbandonata/concluded

Verona April 1980	Gandolfo, piano	LP: Great Operatic Performances GFC 16-17
1993	Unnamed pianist	VHS Video: Bel Canto Society BCS 0115

La rondine, excerpt (Chi il bel sogno di Doretta)

Hilversum December 1968	Netherlands RO Vernizzi	CD: Great Opera Performances GOP 728
Amsterdam March 1972	Netherlands RO Kersjes	LP: Collectors Limited Edition MDP 021 LP: MRF Records MRF 152 LP: Timaclub 21 CD: Fanclub 101

Suor Angelica, excerpt (Senza mamma)

Turin December 1949	EIAR Orchestra Simonetto	78: Cetra BB 25271 LP: Cetra LPC 55011/LPO 2008 CD: Cetra CDO 106 CD: Palladio PD 4162 /Fabbri GVS 06 CD: Great Opera Performances GOP 794 <u>CDO 106 incorrectly dated 1954</u>
Milan December 1958	RAI Milano Orchestra Mannino	LP: Timaclub 30 LP: Rodolphe RP 12438-12439 CD: Cetra CDMR 5020

Il tabarro

Naples May 1960	<u>Role of Giorgetta</u> Verlinghieri, Gismondo San Carlo Orchestra & Chorus Rapalo	Unpublished radio broadcast
Dallas November 1970	Merighi, Bordoni Dallas Civic Opera Orchestra and Chorus Rescigno	Unpublished radio broadcast
Florence December 1970	Bottion, Fioravanti Maggio musicale Orchestra & Chorus Delogù	LP: MRF Records MRF 129 CD: Legato LCD 174

Tosca

Milan October 1957	<u>Role of Tosca</u> Fernandi, Colombo RAI Milano Orchestra & Chorus Tieri	LP: Discocorp RR 514 LP: Movimento musica 02.004

Turin
March 1960
	Misciano,
	Fioravanti
	RAI Torino
	Orchestra & Chorus
	Vernizzi
		CD: Melodram MEL 27025
		VHS Video: Lyric (USA) LCV 016
		VHS Video: Bel Canto Society
		   BCS 0685
		<u>Excerpts</u>
		CD: Rodolphe RPC 32656
		VHS Video: Warner 0630 158983
		VHS Video: Bel Canto Society
		   BCS 0115

Caracas November 1961	Marchiandi, Zagonarta Venezuela SO and Chorus Morelli	Unpublished radio broadcast
Rio de Janeiro July 1964	Labò, Guelfi Teatro Municipal Orchestra & Chorus Molinari-Pradelli	Unpublished radio broadcast
Newark NJ November 1970	Amorim, Shinall New Jersey State Opera Orchestra and Chorus Silipigni	Unpublished radio broadcast
Faenza March 1972	Giacomini, Protti Bologna Communale Orchestra & Chorus Savini	LP: Bongiovanni GAO 166-167 <u>Excerpts</u> LP: Rodolphe RP 12438-12439 CD: Hunt CDHP 607

New York
April 1975
	King, Wixell
	Metropolitan Opera
	Orchestra & Chorus
	Behr
		LP: Historical Recording Enterprises
		   HRE 205
		<u>Excerpts</u>
		LP: Historical Recording Enterprises
		   HRE 203
		<u>Olivero's Metropolitan Opera debut; this
		was not a Metropolitan Opera broadcast</u>

Genova June 1975	Cecchele, Protti Teatro Communale Orchestra & Chorus Molinari-Pradelli	Unpublished radio broadcast
Boston November 1978	Johns, Tozzi Orchestra & Chorus Scott	Unpublished radio broadcast

Tosca/concluded

San Francisco November 1978	Lloveras, Tozzi San Francisco SO and Chorus Peloso	Unpublished radio broadcast
Dallas May 1979	Pavarotti, MacNeil Metropolitan Opera Orchestra & Chorus Conlon	LP: Historical Recording Enterprises HRE 312 Touring performance by Metropolitan Opera

Tosca, Act 3

Amsterdam March 1968	Lega Netherlands RO Vernizzi	LP: Discocorp IGI 303 LP: Collectors Limited Editions MDP 011 CD: Great Opera Performances GOP 728

Tosca, excerpt (Mario! Mario!)

Amsterdam March 1968	Lega Netherlands RO Vernizzi	LP: Discocorp IGI 303 LP: Collectors Limited Edition MDP 011 LP: Timaclub 21 CD: Great Opera Performances GOP 728

Tosca, excerpt (Vissi d'arte)

Turin June 1940	EIAR Orchestra Tansini	78: Cetra BB 25053/CC 2227 LP: Cetra LPC 55015/LPO 2008 LP: Ember GVC 53 CD: Cetra CDO 106 CD: Palladio PD 4162 CD: Andromeda ANR 2536/Fabbri GVS 06 <u>CDO 106 incorrectly dated 1956</u>
Vatican City July 1959	Unidentified accompaniment	LP: Timaclub 21
Amsterdam October 1962	Netherlands RO Vernizzi	LP: Collectors Limited Edition MDP 021 CD: Great Opera Performances GOP 709 CD: Fanclub 101
Florence March 1969	Balducci, piano	CD: Great Opera Performances GOP 717
Marseilles February 1973	Marseilles Opera Orchestra Bazire	CD: Bongiovanni GB 11052
Pistoia March 1973	Gandolfo, piano	CD: Great Opera Performances GOP 795
Trieste October 1975	Silvestri, piano	CD: Eklipse EKR 6
New York October 1979	Ohlsson, piano	LP: Legendary Recordings LR 106
Verona April 1980	Gandolfo, piano	LP: Great Opera Performances GFC 16-17
Vienna May 1981	Schneider, piano	CD: Legato SRO 815

Turandot

Turin September 1938	Role of Liù Cigna, Merli, Neroni, Poli EIAR Orchestra and Chorus Ghione	78: Cetra CC 2066-2081 78: Parlophone R 20410-20425 LP: Cetra N 1206/LPS 3206 LP: Turnabout THS 65049-65050 CD: Cetra CDO 28 CD: Great Opera Performances GOP 794 CD: Arkadia 78016 Excerpts 78: Cetra CB 20517/CB 20049 45: Cetra EPO 0351 LP: Cetra LPC 55015/LPC 55050/ LPO 2008/LPO 2041 LP: Scala (USA) 880 LP: Ember GV 53 LP: Rodolphe RP 12438-12439 CD: Rodolphe RPC 32656 CD: Cetra CDO 106 CD: Palladio PD 4162 CD: Andromeda ANR 2536 CD: Fabbri GVS 06

Turandot, excerpts (Signore ascolta!)

Hilversum December 1968	Netherlands RO Vernizzi	CD: Great Opera Performances GOP 728
Florence March 1969	Balducci, piano	CD: Great Opera Performances GOP 717
Padua April 1971	Corradetti, piano	CD: Myto MCD 93383

Turandot, excerpt (Tu che di gel sei cinta)

Hilversum December 1968	Netherlands RO Vernizzi	CD: Great Opera Performances GOP 728

MAX REGER (1873-1916)

Mariae Wiegenlied

Details not confirmed	Unidentified accompaniment <u>Sung in Italian</u>	LP: Timaclub 21

OTTORINO RESPIGHI (1879-1936)

Navicata

Dallas December 1977	Davis, piano	CD: Legato SRO 815

Nebbie

Dallas December 1977	Davis, piano	CD: Legato SRO 815
Verona April 1980	Gandolfo, piano	LP: Great Opera Performances GFC 16-17
Voghera October 1981	Gandolfo, piano	CD: Great Opera Performances GOP 795

Pioggia

Dallas December 1977	Davis, piano	CD: Legato SRO 815

Stornellatrice

Dallas December 1977	Davis, piano	CD: Legato SRO 815

RENZO ROSSELLINI (1908–1982)

La guerra, dramma in 1 atto

Rome October 1960	Role of Marta Panni, Prandelli, Cesari RAI Roma Orchestra Freccia	CD: Eklipse EKRP 7

GIAOCHINO ROSSINI (1792–1868)

L'invito

Verona April 1980	Gandolfo, piano	LP: Great Operatic Performances GFC 16-17

Petite messe solenelle, excerpt (O salutaris hostia)

Solda August 1976	Montanari, organ	LP: Great Operatic Performances GOP 46 CD: Great Operatic Performances GOP 795

NINO ROTA (1911–1979)

Il capello di paglia di Firenze

Brussels February 1976	Role of Baronessa Devia, Crivellari, Gimenez, Davià Monnaie Orchestra and Chorus Boncompagni	Unpublished radio broadcast

CAMILLE SAINT-SAENS (1835-1921)

Ave Maria

Solda 1985	Montanari, organ	LP: Great Operatic Performances GOP 46 CD: Great Operatic Performances GOP 795

Vicino a te (Samson et Dalila), arrangement by Achilli

Solda 1987	Montanari, organ	LP: Great Operatic Performances GOP 46 CD: Great Operatic Performances GOP 795

FRANZ SCHUBERT (1797-1828)

Ave Maria

Solda August 1978	Montanari, organ <u>Sung in Italian</u>	LP: Great Operatic Performances GOP 46 CD: Great Operatic Performances GOP 795 VHS Video: Bel Canto Society BCS 0115

GIOVANNI SGAMBATI (1841-1914)

Visione

Rome 1957	Unidentified accompaniment	LP: Timaclub 30

ALESSANDRO STRADELLA (1644-1682)

Pietà, signore!

Milan June 1970	Catena, organ	LP: Ariston CLAR 13009 LP: Oscar OSA 148

PIOTR TCHAIKOVSKY (1840–1893)

The Queen of Spades

Florence January 1974	Role of Countess Tagger, Sighele, Fioravanti, Petro Maggio musicale Orchestra & Chorus Kurtz Sung in Italian	Unpublished radio broadcast
Spoleta July 1976	Craig, Borelli, Trussel, Rinaldi Spoleto Festival Orchestra Westminster Choir Ajmone-Marsan Sung in Italian	Unpublished radio broadcast

Mazeppa

Florence June 1954	Role of Maria Radev, Poleri, Bastianini, Christoff Maggio musicale Orchestra & Chorus Perlea Sung in Italian	LP: Rococo 1016 LP: Estro armonico EA 046 LP: Cetra LO 43 CD: Melodram CDM 27070 Estro armonico edition incorrectly described as Turin September 1956

FLAVIO TESTI

La celestina

Florence June 1963	Barbieri, Puglisi, Picchi Maggio musicale Orchestra & Chorus Gavazzeni	Unpublished radio broadcast

PAOLO TOSTI (1846-1916)

Addio

Rome February 1973	Cafaro, piano	LP: Timaclub 10
Pistoia March 1973	Gandolfo, piano	CD: Great Opera Performances GOP 795

Dopo

Rome February 1973	Cafaro, piano	LP: Timaclub 10
Dallas December 1977	Davis, piano	CD: Legato SRO 815

Ideale

New York December 1977	Davis, piano	LP: Legendary Recordings LR 106
Dallas December 1977	Davis, piano	CD: Legato SRO 815

Pour un baiser

Rome February 1973	Cafaro, piano	LP: Timaclub 10
New York December 1977	Davis, piano	LP: Legendary Recordings LR 106
Dallas December 1977	Davis, piano	CD: Legato SRO 815

Il segreto

Rome 1957	Unidentified accompaniment	LP: Collectors Limited Edition MDP 007 LP: Timaclub 30
Pistoia March 1973	Gandolfo, piano	CD: Great Opera Performances GOP 795
Dallas December 1977	Davis, piano	CD: Legato SRO 815

Sogno

Rome February 1973	Cafaro, piano	LP: Timaclub 10
Pistoia March 1973	Gandolfo, piano	CD: Great Opera Performances GOP 795
New York December 1977	Davis, piano	LP: Legendary Recordings LR 106
Dallas December 1977	Davis, piano	CD: Legato SRO 815
Verona April 1980	Gandolfo, piano	LP: Great Operatic Performances GFC 16-17

A version of the song also on VHS Video published by Bel Canto Society BCS 0115

GIUSEPPE VERDI (1813-1901)

Ave Maria, song

Vatican City July 1959	Unidentified accompaniment	LP: Timaclub 21
Florence March 1969	Balducci, piano	CD: Great Opera Performances GOP 717 Track listing suggests that this is Ave Maria from Otello
Solda August 1971	Montanari, organ	LP: Great Operatic Performances GOP 46 CD: Great Operatic Performances GOP 795

La forza del destino, excerpt (Pace, pace, mio Dio!)

Voghera October 1981	Gandolfo, piano	LP: Great Operatic Performances GFC 16-17 LP: Great Operatic Performances GOP 795

Rigoletto, excerpt (Parla! Siam soli!/Tutte le feste/Si vendetta!)

Amsterdam March 1972	Derksen Netherlands RO Kersjes	LP: MRF Records MRF 152 LP: Historical Recording Enterprises HRE 218 LP: Timaclub 19 LP: Rodolophe RP 12438-12439

La traviata, Act 4

Amsterdam May 1967	Antonioli, Protti Netherlands RO Vernizzi	LP: MRF Records MRF 114 LP: Historical Recording Enterprises HRE 218 LP: Morgan MOR 003/AA 100 CD: Verona 28016-28017 CD: Great Opera Performances GOP 709 Excerpts LP: Collectors Limited Edition MDP 007 LP: Discocorp MLG 72 LP: Timaclub 21 CD: Legato LCD 186

La traviata, excerpt (E strano!/Sempre libera)

Turin	Giovagnoli	78: Cetra BB 25034/CC 2225
August 1940	EIAR Orchestra	LP: Cetra LPC 55050/LPO 2008
	Tansini	LP: Collectors Limited Edition MDP 007

LP: Morgan MOR 003
LP: Legendary Recordings LR 210
LP: Rodolphe RP 12438-12439
CD: Rodolphe RPC 32656
CD: Cetra CDO 106
CD: Palladio PD 4162
CD: Andromeda ANR 2536/Fabbri GVS 06
CD: Great Opera Performances GOP 794
<u>CDO 106 incorrectly dated 1953</u>
<u>This recording also used as soundtrack
for a TV performance now published on
VHS Video by Bel Canto Society BCS 0115</u>

La traviata, excerpt (Madamigella Valery?)

Amsterdam	Protti	LP: MRF Records MRF 114
May 1967	Netherlands RO	LP: Historical Recording Enterprises
	Vernizzi	HRE 218

LP: Morgan MOR 003/AA 100
CD: Verona 28016-28017
CD: Great Opera Performances GOP 709

La traviata, excerpt (Amami Alfredo!)

Turin	RAI Torino	78: Cetra AT 0320
May 1953	Orchestra	LP: Cetra LPO 2008
	Basile	LP: OASI 540

LP: Morgan MOR 003
LP: Rodolphe RP 12438-12439
CD: Rodolphe RPC 32656
CD: Cetra CDO 106
CD: Palladio PD 4162
CD: Andromeda ANR 2536
CD: Fabbri GVS 06

VITALINI (Born 1921)

Giaculatorie mariane

Vatican City December 1959	Unidentified accompaniment	LP: Timaclub 21

RICHARD WAGNER (1813-1883)

Tristan und Isolde, excerpt (Mild und leise)

Milan December 1958	RAI Milano Orchestra Mannino Sung in Italian	LP: Timaclub 30 LP: Collectors Limited Edition MDP 021 LP: Discocorp MLG 72 LP: Rodolphe RP 12438-12439 CD: Rodolphe RPC 32656 CD: Melodram MEL 27025 Some issues incorrectly name conductor as Scaglia or incorrectly dated 1963

ERASMUS WIDMANN (1572-1634)

Vergine bella

Solda August 1978	Montanari, organ	LP: Great Operatic Performances GOP 46 LP: Great Operatic Performances GOP 795

ERMANNO WOLF-FERRARI (1876-1948)

I quattro rusteghi

Turin December 1969	Adani, Barbieri, Lazari, Mariotti, Rossi-Lemeni Teatro Regio Orchestra & Chorus Gracis	Unpublished radio broadcast

RICCARDO ZANDONAI (1883-1944)

Francesca da Rimini

Milan June 1959	<u>Role of Francesca</u> Del Monaco, Malaspina La Scala Orchestra & Chorus Gavazzeni	LP: MRF Records MRF 114 LP: Estro armonico EA 041 LP: Replica RPL 2451-2453 CD: Legato LCD 186

**Francesca da Rimini, excerpts (E' ancora sgombro il campo del comune?;
No, Smaragdi, no!; Paolo, datemi pace!; Ah la parola che i miei occhi
incontranto!)**

Monte Carlo April-May 1969	Del Monaco, Carbonari Monte Carlo Opera Orchestra Rescigno	LP: Decca SET 422 CD: Decca 433 0332

Francesca da Rimini, excerpts (Ora andate/E così vada s'è pur mio destino!)

Amsterdam May 1967	Antonioli, Protti Netherlands RO Vernizzi	CD: Verona 28016-28017 CD: Great Opera Performances GOP 709
Monte Carlo April-May 1969	Del Monaco, Carbonari Monte Carlo Opera Orchestra Rescigno	LP: Decca SET 422 CD: Decca 433 0332

Francesca da Rimini, excerpt (Paolo, datemi pace!)

Padua April 1971	Corradetti, piano	CD: Myto MCD 93383

<u>Published speech interviews with Magda Olivero can be heard on the LPs Tima
10, Tima 30 and Rodolphe RP 12438-12439 (all in Italian); she also provides
spoken commentary to the video film "The Art of Singing" (Warner 0603 158983),
in which she is also seen in stage performance (see under Tosca)</u>
<u>Various interview fragments also on video published by Bel Canto Society BCS 0115</u>

Discographies

Teachers and pupils
Schwarzkopf / Ivogün / Cebotari /
Seinemeyer / Welitsch / Streich / Berger
7 separate discographies, 400 pages

The post-war German tradition
Kempe / Keilberth / Sawallisch /Kubelik /
Cluytens
5 separate discographies, 300 pages

**Mid-century conductors
and More Viennese singers**
Böhm / De Sabata / Knappertsbusch / Serafin /
Krauss / Dermota / Rysanek / Wächter /
Reining / Kunz
10 separate discographies, 420 pages

Leopold Stokowski
Discography and concert register, 300 pages

Tenors in a lyric tradition
Fritz Wunderlich / Walther Ludwig /
Peter Anders
3 separate discographies, 350 pages

Makers of the Philharmonia
Galliera / Susskind / Kletzki / Malko / Matacic /
Dobrowen / Kurtz / Fistoulari
8 separate discographies, 300 pages

A notable quartet
Janowitz / Ludwig / Gedda / Fischer-Dieskau
4 separate discographies, 600 pages

Hungarians in exile
Reiner / Dorati /Szell
3 separate discographies, 300 pages

The art of the diva
Muzio / Callas / Olivero
3 separate discographies, 225 pages

The lyric baritone
Reinmar / Hüsch / Metternich / Uhde /
Wächter
5 separate discographies, 225 pages

Price £22 per volume (£28 outside UK)
*Special offer any 3 volumes for
£55 (£75 outside UK)*
Postage included
Order from: John Hunt, Flat 6,
37 Chester Way, London SE11 4UR

Credits

Valuable help with the supply of
information or illustration material
for these discographies came from:

John Ardoin, Dallas
Mike Ashman, Ware
Ray Burford, Sony Classical London
Richard Chlupaty, London
Clifford Elkin, Glasgow
Bill Flowers, London
Michael Gray, Alexandria VA
Syd Gray, Hove
Paul Gunther, Minnesota Orchestra
Bill Holland, Polygram London
Ken Jagger, EMI Classics London
Roderick Krüsemann, Amsterdam
Luis Luna, Berlin
Alan Newcombe, DG Hamburg
John Raymon, London
Phil Rees, Pewsey
Malcolm Walker, Harrow

Discographies by Travis & Emery:

Discographies by John Hunt.

1987: 978-1-906857-14-1: From Adam to Webern: the Recordings of von Karajan.

1991: 978-0-951026-83-0: 3 Italian Conductors and 7 Viennese Sopranos: 10 Discographies: Arturo Toscanini, Guido Cantelli, Carlo Maria Giulini, Elisabeth Schwarzkopf, Irmgard Seefried, Elisabeth Gruemmer, Sena Jurinac, Hilde Gueden, Lisa Della Casa, Rita Streich.

1992: 978-0-951026-85-4: Mid-Century Conductors and More Viennese Singers: 10 Discographies: Karl Boehm, Victor De Sabata, Hans Knappertsbusch, Tullio Serafin, Clemens Krauss, Anton Dermota, Leonie Rysanek, Eberhard Waechter, Maria Reining, Erich Kunz.

1993: 978-0-951026-87-8: More 20th Century Conductors: 7 Discographies: Eugen Jochum, Ferenc Fricsay, Carl Schuricht, Felix Weingartner, Josef Krips, Otto Klemperer, Erich Kleiber.

1994: 978-0-951026-88-5: Giants of the Keyboard: 6 Discographies: Wilhelm Kempff, Walter Gieseking, Edwin Fischer, Clara Haskil, Wilhelm Backhaus, Artur Schnabel.

1994: 978-0-951026-89-2: Six Wagnerian Sopranos: 6 Discographies: Frieda Leider, Kirsten Flagstad, Astrid Varnay, Martha Moedl, Birgit Nilsson, Gwyneth Jones.

1995: 978-0-952582-70-0: Musical Knights: 6 Discographies: Henry Wood, Thomas Beecham, Adrian Boult, John Barbirolli, Reginald Goodall, Malcolm Sargent.

1995: 978-0-952582-71-7: A Notable Quartet: 4 Discographies: Gundula Janowitz, Christa Ludwig, Nicolai Gedda, Dietrich Fischer-Dieskau.

1996: 978-0-952582-72-4: The Post-War German Tradition: 5 Discographies: Rudolf Kempe, Joseph Keilberth, Wolfgang Sawallisch, Rafael Kubelik, Andre Cluytens.

1996: 978-0-952582-73-1: Teachers and Pupils: 7 Discographies: Elisabeth Schwarzkopf, Maria Ivoguen, Maria Cebotari, Meta Seinemeyer, Ljuba Welitsch, Rita Streich, Erna Berger.

1996: 978-0-952582-77-9: Tenors in a Lyric Tradition: 3 Discographies: Peter Anders, Walther Ludwig, Fritz Wunderlich.

1997: 978-0-952582-78-6: The Lyric Baritone: 5 Discographies: Hans Reinmar, Gerhard Huesch, Josef Metternich, Hermann Uhde, Eberhard Waechter.

1997: 978-0-952582-79-3: Hungarians in Exile: 3 Discographies: Fritz Reiner, Antal Dorati, George Szell.

1997: 978-1-901395-00-6: The Art of the Diva: 3 Discographies: Claudia Muzio, Maria Callas, Magda Olivero.

1997: 978-1-901395-01-3: Metropolitan Sopranos: 4 Discographies: Rosa Ponselle, Eleanor Steber, Zinka Milanov, Leontyne Price.

1997: 978-1-901395-02-0: Back From The Shadows: 4 Discographies: Willem Mengelberg, Dimitri Mitropoulos, Hermann Abendroth, Eduard Van Beinum.

1997: 978-1-901395-03-7: More Musical Knights: 4 Discographies: Hamilton Harty, Charles Mackerras, Simon Rattle, John Pritchard.

1998: 978-1-901395-94-5: Conductors On The Yellow Label: 8 Discographies: Fritz Lehmann, Ferdinand Leitner, Ferenc Fricsay, Eugen Jochum, Leopold Ludwig, Artur Rother, Franz Konwitschny, Igor Markevitch.

1998: 978-1-901395-95-2: More Giants of the Keyboard: 5 Discographies: Claudio Arrau, Gyorgy Cziffra, Vladimir Horowitz, Dinu Lipatti, Artur Rubinstein.

1998: 978-1-901395-96-9: Mezzo and Contraltos: 5 Discographies: Janet Baker, Margarete Klose, Kathleen Ferrier, Giulietta Simionato, Elisabeth Hoengen.

Discography by Stephen J. Pettitt, edited by John Hunt:

Available from: Travis & Emery at 17 Cecil Court, London, UK. (+44) 20 7 240 2129. email on sales@travis-and-emery.com .

Music and Books published by Travis & Emery Music Bookshop:

Anon.: Hymnarium Sarisburiense, cum Rubricis et Notis Musicis.

Agricola, Johann Friedrich from Tosi: Anleitung zur Singkunst.

Bach, C.P.E.: edited W. Emery: Nekrolog or Obituary Notice of J.S. Bach.

Bateson, Naomi Judith: Alcock of Salisbury

Bathe, William: A Briefe Introduction to the Skill of Song

Bax, Arnold: Symphony #5, Arranged for Piano Four Hands by Walter Emery

Burney, Charles: The Present State of Music in France and Italy

Burney, Charles: The Present State of Music in Germany, The Netherlands ...

Burney, Charles: An Account of the Musical Performances ... Handel

Burney, Karl: Nachricht von Georg Friedrich Handel's Lebensumstanden.

Cobbett, W.W.: Cobbett's Cyclopedic Survey of Chamber Music. (2 vols.)

Corrette, Michel: Le Maitre de Clavecin

Crimp, Bryan: Dear Mr. Rosenthal ... Dear Mr. Gaisberg ...

Crimp, Bryan: Solo: The Biography of Solomon

d'Indy, Vincent: Beethoven: Biographie Critique

d'Indy, Vincent: Beethoven: A Critical Biography

d'Indy, Vincent: César Franck (in French)

Frescobaldi, Girolamo: D'Arie Musicali per Cantarsi. Primo & Secondo Libro.

Geminiani, Francesco: The Art of Playing the Violin.

Handel; Purcell; Boyce; Geene et al: Calliope or English Harmony: Volume First.

Hawkins, John: A General History of the Science and Practice of Music (5 vols.)

Herbert-Caesari, Edgar: The Science and Sensations of Vocal Tone

Herbert-Caesari, Edgar: Vocal Truth

Hopkins and Rimboult: The Organ. Its History and Construction.

Hunt, John: Adam to Webern: the recordings of von Karajan

Isaacs, Lewis: Hänsel and Gretel. A Guide to Humperdinck's Opera.

Isaacs, Lewis: Königskinder (Royal Children) A Guide to Humperdinck's Opera.

Lacassagne, M. l'Abbé Joseph : Traité Général des élémens du Chant.

Lascelles (née Catley), Anne: The Life of Miss Anne Catley.

Mainwaring, John: Memoirs of the Life of the Late George Frederic Handel

Malcolm, Alexander: A Treaty of Music: Speculative, Practical and Historical

Marx, Adolph Bernhard: Die Kunst des Gesanges, Theoretisch-Practisch

May, Florence: The Life of Brahms

Mellers, Wilfrid: Angels of the Night: Popular Female Singers of Our Time

Mellers, Wilfrid: Bach and the Dance of God

Mellers, Wilfrid: Beethoven and the Voice of God

Travis & Emery Music Bookshop
17 Cecil Court, London, WC2N 4EZ, United Kingdom.
Tel. (+44) 20 7240 2129

Music and Books published by Travis & Emery Music Bookshop:

Mellers, Wilfrid: Caliban Reborn - Renewal in Twentieth Century Music
Mellers, Wilfrid: François Couperin and the French Classical Tradition
Mellers, Wilfrid: Harmonious Meeting
Mellers, Wilfrid: Le Jardin Retrouvé, The Music of Frederic Mompou
Mellers, Wilfrid: Music and Society, England and the European Tradition
Mellers, Wilfrid: Music in a New Found Land: ... ... American Music
Mellers, Wilfrid: Romanticism and the Twentieth Century (from 1800)
Mellers, Wilfrid: The Masks of Orpheus: ...... the Story of European Music.
Mellers, Wilfrid: The Sonata Principle (from c. 1750)
Mellers, Wilfrid: Vaughan Williams and the Vision of Albion
Panchianio, Cattuffio: Rutzvanscad Il Giovine
Pearce, Charles: Sims Reeves, Fifty Years of Music in England.
Playford, John: An Introduction to the Skill of Musick.
Purcell, Henry et al: Harmonia Sacra ... The First Book, (1726)
Purcell, Henry et al: Harmonia Sacra ... Book II (1726)
Quantz, Johann: Versuch einer Anweisung die Flöte traversiere zu spielen.
Rameau, Jean-Philippe: Code de Musique Pratique, ou Methodes.
Rastall, Richard: The Notation of Western Music.
Rimbault, Edward: The Pianoforte, Its Origins, Progress, and Construction.
Rousseau, Jean Jacques: Dictionnaire de Musique
Rubinstein, Anton : Guide to the proper use of the Pianoforte Pedals.
Sainsbury, John S.: Dictionary of Musicians. Vol. 1. (1825). 2 vols.
Simpson, Christopher: A Compendium of Practical Musick in Five Parts
Spohr, Louis: Autobiography
Spohr, Louis: Grand Violin School
Tans'ur, William: A New Musical Grammar; or The Harmonical Spectator
Terry, Charles Sanford: Four-Part Chorals of J.S. Bach. (German & English)
Terry, Charles Sanford: Joh. Seb. Bach, Cantata Texts, Sacred and Secular.
Terry, Charles Sanford: The Origins of the Family of Bach Musicians.
Tosi, Pierfrancesco: Opinioni de' Cantori Antichi, e Moderni
Van der Straeten, Edmund: History of the Violoncello, The Viol da Gamba ...
Van der Straeten, Edmund: History of the Violin, Its Ancestors... (2 vols.)
Walther, J. G.: Musicalisches Lexikon ober Musicalische Bibliothec

Travis & Emery Music Bookshop
17 Cecil Court, London, WC2N 4EZ, United Kingdom.
Tel. (+44) 20 7240 2129

CPSIA information can be obtained at www.ICGtesting.com
Printed in the USA
LVOW030931301011

252665LV00003B/53/P